Sybil Canac | Renée Grimaud | Katia Thomas

111 Places
in Paris
That You
Shouldn't Miss

emons:

© Emons Verlag GmbH
All rights reserved
© for photographs: see page 239
© Cover motif: iStockphoto.com/levkr
English translation: Hadley Suter
Design: Eva Kraskes, based on a design
by Lübbeke | Naumann | Thoben
Maps: altancicek.design, www.altancicek.de
Printing and binding: Hitzegrad Print Medien & Service –
Lensing Druck Gruppe, Feldbachacker 16, 44149 Dortmund
Printed in Germany 2017
ISBN 978-3-7408-0159-5

Original title: *111 lieux absolument étonnants à Paris*
© Hachette Livre (Hachette Tourisme) 2016

Did you enjoy it? Do you want more?
Join us in uncovering new places around the world at:
www.111places.com

Foreword

It is called the most beautiful city in the world, and the more than thirty million tourists that visit it each year seem to agree. When they first discover the City of Lights, they come armed with a list of monuments – the ones that make Paris, Paris. Accordingly, they march from the Champs-Élysées to the Eiffel Tower; they wander through the Louvre; they hike up Montmartre to Sacré-Cœur Cathedral.

The tourists of Paris, won over by the enchanting atmosphere of the capital, just cannot stop coming back. Finally, they realize that the magic of Paris is not *just* these symbolic sites. It is stumbling upon a little-known garden one morning before anyone else; it is looking up to notice the quirky façades that peek out from venerable Haussmann buildings; it is having a coffee in a historical place that has been touched up by a trendy architect. Make the same trip a year or two later and you can bet you will realize just how much the neighborhood has changed since your last visit.

To conjure up a list of the most amazing places in Paris is an exhilarating exercise – because it is never finished! In constantly pacing the streets of the city, in keeping up with everything that keeps evolving, it becomes clear that this is a city that reveals itself with enormous generosity – especially in places off the beaten track. Even when you have lived there for decades, there is always some detail you have never noticed.

The tourists who really fall in love with Paris find themselves in the exact same situation: as their visits start to rack up, their interest sharpens, and their perception too. And the more idiosyncrasies they discover, the more they hone their science of the City of Lights, until it appears in all its intimacy and richness, from its origins until this century that keeps transforming its contours. Perhaps on their next visit, Paris will no longer be a chimera, but a reality.

Renée Grimaud

111 Places

1 Adzak Museum-Workshop
The home of an illusion artist

The fate of Royston Wright, otherwise known as Roy Adzak, was a strange one. Born in England in 1928, he was an engineer, sculptor, painter, photographer, and globetrotter. During archaeological digs in Afghanistan, he noticed that when the sun hit the concave curves of pottery, it gave the illusion of convex reliefs. Adzak spent the rest of his life trying to recreate this optical illusion. In 1962, not far from Montparnasse, he moved into an old house with a garden and a garage that would be his atelier. Twenty years later, he built it up into a building of four floors. At the top of the façade, he put the casting of his head and on the ground, the imprint of his hands.

Since 1955, Adzak worked on prints, fossilizations, and other "negative objects" – concave designs in anthropomorphic or otherwise nature-inspired forms. He also plastered living models. His atelier contains his own mummified body, wrapped in medical bandages and plaster, along with other astonishing works: columns supporting silhouettes in relief and counter-relief, prints of human body parts, animal and vegetable dehydrations, a pyramid containing the cadaver of a raven.

During his lifetime, his work was shown by well-known gallerists such as Iris Clert. But the artist who'd worked on the traces of time was its first victim. Adzak often practiced complicated medical techniques on himself – which is how he died in 1987 at the age of 59. Buried in the Montparnasse cemetery, his grave is crowned with a little pyramid where you can see his reflection. His atelier and his house have remained intact. The little garden is home to ceramic chickens, owls, and cats by his nephew Nicholas Wright. His house is occupied by artists in residence.

Adzak's friend and fellow Brit Margaret Crowther created the museum thirty years ago, and today organizes art shows and poetry readings in the space.

Address 3 Rue Jonquoy, 75014 Paris, +33 (0)1 45 43 01 98 or +33 (0)9 61 23 20 91 | Getting there Metro to Plaisance (Line 13) | Hours Sun 3pm–9pm and by appointment. Free entry. | Tip In the Plaisance neighborhood, at number 19bis Rue Jonquoy, you can also find the home and atelier of the artist Zao Wou-Ki. The great Chinese painter, who died in 2013 at the age of 93, lived there from 1960 to 2011.

2 The Animal Cemetery

A pet cemetery for the dearly departed

Seeing the number of people who come to pay homage to their departed pets, leaving a bouquet of flowers or a little souvenir, you may be surprised to find yourself moved to the point of forgetting that you are not in a human cemetery. Besides dogs, which take up most of the plots, many other creatures have lucked into this chic final resting place: cats, birds, rabbits, hamsters, fish, horses, and even a monkey.

The names on the epitaphs attest to the affection that their owners felt for them: Bibi, Fury, Tendresse, B.b., Veinard, Pupuce, Sultan, Mouchette, etc. There's even one headstone expressing the love of a mother for her dog Loulou, who saved her child from drowning in the Garonne River in 1985.

There are also some animal celebrities here: Rintintin, the valiant young hero of the TV series of the same name; Prince of Wales, who appeared 406 times on stage at the Théâtre du Gymnase in 1905 and 1906 (as you can read on his epitaph). Then there is Barry, who belonged to the monks of the Hospice du Grand-Saint-Bernard. On the monument erected at the entrance of the cemetery, the inscription references the legend according to which "after saving the lives of 40 people, [Barry] was killed by the 41st."

The cemetery came into being at the end of the 19th century thanks to two animal-lovers: Georges Harmois, a publicist, and Marguerite Durand, the founder of the newspaper *La Fronde*. Until then, the bodies of departed pets were tossed in the trash or in the Seine. On June 21, 1898, a law was passed allowing pets to be buried "in a grave situated as often as possible one hundred meters from the dwellings of their masters and in such a way that the cadaver would be covered by a layer of earth having at least one meter of thickness." The only condition was that the tombs not resemble human graves. Since then, we may have forgotten this rule a bit!

Il sauva la vie
à 40 personnes
il fut tué par la 41ème!

(Gd S. Bernard)

Address 4 Pont de Clichy, 92600 Asnières-sur-Seine, +33 (0)1 40 86 21 11 | Getting there Metro to Gabriel Péri (Line 13) or RER to Gare d'Asnières-sur-Seine | Hours Every day but Mon, Mar 16–Oct 15, 10am–6pm; off-season 10am–4:30pm. Closed for all holidays except Nov 1. | Tip On the platform at the foot of the cemetery you can hop on a boat that will take you down the Seine – with music! – all the way to Saint-Cloud and back. It is a great way to discover the banks of the river and Île de la Jatte and its "Temple of Love" (Temple de l'Amour, www.tourisme92.com).

3 _ Anis Gras Cultural Center
A liqueur with history

For those who've tried it, Anis Gras is a Proustian liqueur evocative of nostalgic memories, because it is no longer made in the red brick factory whose long wall borders one of the main streets of Arcueil. Remaining almost perfectly intact, the factory was constructed by the initiative of Émile Raspail in the 1870s. This Paris-trained engineer was the son of François-Vincent Raspail, the socialist deputy and biologist-doctor who gave his name to the famous boulevard in Paris. He devoted himself in service to the poor and ultimately invented a curative camphor-based digestive liqueur.

When Émile Raspail took over, he placed the factory right next to his house in Arcueil to better run the place. The factory kept growing to over 40,000 square feet, reaching all the way to the corner of Avenue Laplace and Rue Lénine.

Émile Raspail was mayor of the city from 1878 until his death in 1887, and he left his mark on the city, bringing it a great number of modern constructions. After his death, his family continued his work for some time before selling the business to the Erven Lucas Bols establishment, producers of "hygienic" liqueurs. It wasn't until 1963 that the famous Frères Gras arrived, who commercialized the long-reputed Anis Gras anisette.

The factory, bought back by the town in 1981, was given to the association "Le lieu de l'autre" in 2005. The entry pavilion, the orangery, the beautiful glass window walls, and the old ateliers were well-conserved and now house a number of avant-garde artists. The beautiful industrial property is coming back to life with performances, exhibitions, concerts, and other events, not to mention a cafeteria that serves up its specialties every Friday from noon to 2:00pm: a house couscous dish and irresistible pastries washed down with a nice mint tea. Attention all foodies: reservations are required!

Address 55 Avenue Laplace, 94110 Arcueil, +33 (0)1 49 12 03 29, www.lelieudelautre.com | **Getting there** RER to Laplace | **Tip** At 52 Avenue Laplace, you will find the chapel of the Immaculate Conception Franciscan nuns (*les franciscaines de l'Immaculée Conception*). Also known as the Auguste-Perret chapel, it was built by the Perret brotherhood between 1927 and 1929 and is a beautiful example of modern architecture. It was landmarked in 1999. Masses on Sundays and visits on heritage days (you can look up the yearly calendar of *les journées du patrimoine*).

4_ The AntiCafé Beaubourg

Here's to spending time together

Sometimes, ideas come to us from faraway places. In this case, it was a young man of Ukrainian descent who brought to Paris a simple but ingenious concept that is all the rage in Russia – the anticafé, where you pay not for goods consumed, but for the time spent on the premises.

In 2013, piggybacking off the success of the "sharing economy," Leonid Goncharov launched the AntiCafé Beaubourg, a coworking space where you can work and meet other people. The AntiCafé is meant to feel like home: you can open the fridge and grab a yogurt, make yourself a hot drink, or even bring a meal from your own kitchen. Wish to take out a book from the library? No problem. Newspapers? Also available to clients who can use the space to hang out, chat, and make friends. The walls are covered in classified ads where you just might find happiness. Once night falls, it is time to party. Their program is varied: films, concerts, social games. You can curl up on the couches, sway in a rocking chair, or just sit in a normal chair anywhere in the beautiful vaulted room.

But for optimal productivity, you need not only comfort but space and light. Leonid and his friends from BonkersLab, specialists in product design and interior layout, designed AntiCafé in light colors with a witty "Welcome home!" message painted on the wall. The furniture was either scored at flea markets, Emmaüs charity shops (a very trendy approach), or created specially for the space.

The project was such a hit that AntiCafé has since opened smaller-scale spin-offs. The AntiCafé Louvre, on rue de Richelieu, is in the heart of the city. The most recent, "the big one," is AntiCafé Innovation. As its name indicates, the creators had lofty goals for this location: it is within the Campus Cluster Paris Innovation, a group that brings together scholars, techies, start-ups, and big business.

Address 79 Rue Quincampoix, 75003 Paris, www.anticafe.eu | Getting there Metro to Rambuteau (Line 11) | Hours Mon–Fri 9am–10pm; Sat & Sun 10am–9pm | Tip The AntiCafé Louvre is open during the same hours as the AntiCafé Beaubourg (10 Rue de Richelieu, 75001 Paris, +33 (0)1 73 71 72 86). The AntiCafé Olympiades, 59 Rue National, in the bustling 13th arrondissement, is only open Mon–Fri 8am–6:30pm.

5 Arcade Street

The temple of old-school video games

Video game destination of those in the know, Arcade Street is one of the two remaining Japanese-style arcades in Paris. Created in 2010 by Anatole Albar, the place is a real survivor. Over 4,000 square feet of street-level and basement space, Albar has created an underground ambiance in what was once the site of a 200-horsepower steam generator that powered the street's 230 ateliers.

Albar's décor fits into the neighborhood vibe: street art on the walls, along with other artworks created by friends, and a metal staircase encased in an overhead chain-link fencing of *arcades* (a little joke Albar made to himself – in French, the word also means "archways").

On the lower level you see the stone walls of the original cellar, and you can spot another stairway to a second, deeper basement that leads to an underground passage to the other side of the street: this was the passageway of the steam generator's drive shaft.

In the nineties, arcade games were all the rage before becoming pale adaptations of themselves destined for video game consoles.

Here in this pasture of solitary gaming, 150 people can play at the same time. Arcade Street has relaunched still-popular combat games like Street Fighter 4, The King of Fighters, and all the big series of VS Fighting!

Along with a "hit parade" of the most in-demand games, you can find old gems of every type: shoot-'em-up games like Darius Burst; beat-'em-all options like Metal Slug, rhythm games (*jeux de "Tam tam"* in French) like *Taiko no Tatsujin*; dance games like Dance Dance Revolution; and of course classics like Pacman and Mario Kart.

A group of mostly 18- to 35-year-olds come after school or work for a bit of guilt-free fun. The arcade gets rowdy and pretty loud. For its devotees, there's no doubt: you're tackling both games and other gamers, so emotions run higher than at home on a console or online.

Address 10 Rue des Immeubles-Industriels, 75011 Paris, +33 (0)1 40 09 85 71, www.arcadestreet.fr | Getting there Metro to Nation (Lines 1, 2, 6, and 9) | Hours Mon 5pm–10pm; Tues–Sat 2pm–5pm | Tip On Place de l'Île-de-la-Réunion, facing the rue des Colonnes-du-Trône, is a plaque explaining that a guillotine was installed here during the French Revolution on June 13, 1794. The communal graves are not far off in the Picpus Cemetery.

6__ The Armenian Cafeteria

Armenian soul food

It does the soul good to visit places that buzz with foreign accents. The cafeteria at the Maison de la culture arménienne (Armenian cultural center) is one of those. Invisible from the street, it is an address for those in the know. After pushing open a heavy door, you cross a tree-lined courtyard and climb a few steps before entering a beautiful room draped in flags, fashionable photos, and paintings from the 1950s.

As soon as you enter, the owner Tchinar welcomes you as if you were family. She tells you about the specials, all of which are mouthwatering: beef ravioli in two varieties (the small ones are Russian, the bigger ones Georgian) served with crème fraîche, stuffed eggplant, and Caucasian chicken kabobs.

Meanwhile, her husband Mamikon keeps busy in the kitchen. As soon as you sit down, things start to appear at the table: lavash breads, a plate of marinated vegetables and a salad, all on the house. The dishes themselves are generously portioned for the modesty of the prices. If you ask nicely and there is not too much of a crowd, Tchinar will hang around your table to tell you about her life in her native Tbilisi.

In this cafeteria where the entire Armenian community comes to hang out – Saturdays, especially, they come with their whole families – you will find yourself very quickly adopted and you will probably vow to come back soon. A regular reads his newspaper in one corner. In another there is a couple playing cards, while nearby a table of six people wait to be served.

This part of the 9th arrondissement around the Cadet metro station and by rue de Trévise, formerly known as Little Armenia (*la petite Arménie*), welcomed many Armenians after the genocide of 1915. The Maison de la culture arménienne has been around for more than sixty years, bringing together the community around common projects. There are language classes, folk dancing, and even a choir.

Address 17 Rue Bleue, 75009 Paris, +33 (0)1 48 24 63 89 | **Getting there** Metro to Cadet (Line 7) | **Hours** Mon–Sat noon–3pm and 7pm–11pm. On Saturday nights, call to make a reservation. Daily specials €12. | **Tip** If you want to try another country, I wholeheartedly recommend the restaurant Boukhoura, 37 Rue de Trévise. In a gorgeous room filled with artisanal objects, you can try traditional cuisine from Uzbekistan.

7 Arts et Métiers Station

A dream bubble

The RATP Parisian transport system should really put out calls to comic strip artists to redesign their Metro stations. They would have a certain cachet, believe me! It sort of feels like that on the line 11 platforms of the Arts et Métiers station.

It is a total dream world. Sort of like a cross between Jules Verne and François Schuiten, the Belgian artist behind *Les Cités Obscures* (The Obscure Cities). Or maybe it is more like being in the Nautilus from *20,000 Leagues Under the Sea*. Close your eyes, then open them again slowly. Can't you see it? Just like being in a submarine.

Created in 1994 for the bicentennial celebration of the Conservatoire National des Arts et Métiers, the station is entirely covered in copper – even its vaulted archways. It is a tribute to the technical and industrial heritage of the Conservatory, as are the enormous gearwheels on the ceilings, which also hint at the many constructed-themed works on exhibit in the nearby Arts et Métiers museum.

On the platforms of the station, porthole windows showcase models of the armillary sphere – an instrument modeling the celestial sphere – of the American satellite Telstar. That was the first communication satellite, which was launched in 1962 from the hydraulic wheel, and later from the Pont Antoinette in the Midi-Pyrénées region in France. The museum is worth checking out not only for the works themselves, but for the history tidbits you're sure to come away with.

All the decorative elements – the station's nameplates, its seats, even its trash cans – were created out of copper so as to stay in the unique tone of the ensemble. Linking Châtelet to the *mairie* of Les Lilas in Seine-Saint-Denis, line 11 is, at 4 miles, the shortest of the Parisian Metro lines and one of the least used. It was also one of the last to be put into service, in 1935. But how many other lines get to boast a station like this one?

Address Rue Réaumur and Rue Turbigo, 75003 Paris | Tip With its neon-colored ceilings, black-lacquer bar, mosaic-tiled floors, and geometrical lines of the 1950s, Le Parisien is a great place to grab food or just a drink until late at night. (337 Rue Saint-Martin, 75003 Paris, Mon – Fri 8am – 2am; Sat 10am – 2am; Sun 10am – 6pm)

8 Baguett's Café
A no-frills coffee shop

Back to the simple pleasures, the authentic ones! Eating a good baguette toasted with butter is one of the greatest luxuries. If the crust happens to be nice and crunchy, and the butter salted – it is the ne plus ultra! Nothing better in the world. For all nostalgic fans of the "real" baguette, this little spot opened in 2015, right nearby the Comédie-Française and the Palais-Royal Gardens. It is run by Amando and Jeanne, a former model who today bakes scrumptious pastries based on recipes taught to her by her grandmother.

As soon as you're in the door, the delicious smells are overwhelming: the smell of fresh bread, but also of *pains au chocolat*, croissants, shortbread, and several other cakes meant for one thing and one thing only – to be eaten.

With its "Franglais" name, Baguett's Café has deliberately chosen a friendly, congenial vibe: its banquettes upholstered in burlap coffee bags inscribed in different languages; its tables of unfinished wood; its walls left un-retouched. The space has a roomy feel thanks to its mirrors and many lamps, which come from Jeanne and Amando's travels worldwide.

The bread? The baguettes are made by the bakery L'Essentiel, which also makes the two-foot-long ciabatta that are cut into sandwiches at lunchtime. Coffee comes from Verlet, a nearby boutique merchant. And if coffee's not your thing, you can order a hot chocolate or a Dammann Frères tea. The mouth-watering Francis Miot jams are presented in pretty little glass jars, like those used to sterilize foie gras, or duck livers.

In the open kitchen, Jeanne bakes lemon tarts, Parisian custards, sponge cakes, and her special invention, la Jeannett's – a little gluten-free pastry. At Baguett's Café, the baguette is a mainstay of breakfast, lunch and the afternoon snack, *le goûter*. Many of these tempting options can be seen displayed in the storefront window.

Address 33 Rue de Richelieu, 75001 Paris | **Getting there** Metro to Pyramides (Lines 7 and 14) or Palais Royal – Musée du Louvre (Lines 1 and 7) | **Hours** Tue – Sat 8:30am – 6:30pm; Sun 9:30am – 3pm | **Tip** Cross the street and open the door to a charming home décor boutique with a quirky name, featuring trays, notebooks, jewelry, carved-wood stools, and sumptuous kimonos. It is called Le facteur n'est pas passé (The mailman didn't come) (20 Rue de Richelieu, +33 (0)1 42 61 11 22, Mon – Fri noon – 7pm, Sat 2:30pm – 7pm).

9 Le Balcon Restaurant
Paris in all of its (phil)harmony

Go see Paris from above! It is an enchanting 180-degree view that spans from the Eiffel Tower to the Grands Moulins de Pantin and including La Défense. Right beneath you there's La Géode and La Cité des Sciences et de l'Industrie (the biggest science museum in Europe). You can see it all from the terrace of Le Balcon – which is accessible at all hours, and is even more beautiful at night when Paris is bathed in sparkling lights!

Music lovers did not take long to adopt this distinctive restaurant. Its décor is mostly black, speckled in bright yellow on the ceiling, and decked out in autumnal armchairs in rich hues of golden brown, green, and red.

As for the food, there's something for everyone, and at every price point. Those in a hurry might go for the charcuterie board – choose from Iberian, Italian, or French – or else a cheese platter from Jean-Yves Bordier. Or maybe you would prefer the fresh cod fish and chips, or the Balcon Burger, which is made with Charolais beef and which has attracted a devoted fan base. Those who have more time might choose the wild cod or the *volaille d'Ancenis*, a signature dish of Karil Lopez, the young chef who cut his teeth under Michel Rostang at L'Absinthe before joining Éric Frechon at the Hôtel Bristol.

The menu might seem simple at first glance, but all the dishes are remarkably finessed and inventive. The night I was there, I loved the roasted cod with chorizo emulsion and house purée. For dessert, I followed it up with a citrus aspic *au muscat*, which was light and had a great mix of flavors.

When you make your reservation, ask for a table near the big bay windows, and if you want to enjoy this exquisite panorama of Paris while feeling like you are all alone in the restaurant, ask specifically for table 107, which is very private. If you want to book an event with family or friends, no problem – private areas are reserved for just that.

Address 221 Avenue Jean-Jaurès, 75019 Paris, +33 (0)1 40 32 30 01, www.restaurant-lebalcon.fr | Getting there Metro to Hoche (Line 5); direct access from the Q-Park Philharmonie parking lot via elevator | Hours Tue–Sun from 6:30pm, reservations necessary | Tip Right near the wall of the Parc de la Villette, go see the Fontaine aux Lios de Nubie, at its prettiest at night when it is lit up. Known as the first fountain that could spray water, in the 19th century it decorated the Place du Château d'Eau, or what is now the Place de la République.

10__Le Bar à Bulles

Daydream in peace

In French, the word for "bubbles" (*les bulles*) can also be used as a verb: *buller*, or, to veg out completely.

To find the Bar à Bulles, the easiest way is to get to the Moulin Rouge. From there, take the stairs to your left. You will hesitate, you will wondering what kind of shady bar you're headed towards. Once at the top of the steps… Nope, not there yet! After following a long wooden counter, you will enter a huge room, full of light, decked out in 1950s furniture and tiling, and a ceiling hung with colorful lampshades.

The surprises do not end there. The big bay window looks out onto a green terrace, open summer through winter, except in heavy rain, where there are at least a dozen tables waiting to be grabbed.

The café's name suddenly makes sense: to be able to "bubble" for hours in a spot like this… heaven! In the main room, there's a cozy little nook in one corner, a comfy couch in another, and the space is big enough to not be bothered by others. Here Stéphane Vatinel, who's also the director of the REcyclerie and the Pavillon des Canaux, has put into practice the "coffice" concept – "coffee plus office" – that is all the rage and responds to the needs of thirty-somethings, the majority of its clientele.

In short, the idea is to let you drink a good coffee while tapping away at a laptop as if you were at the office. Only you're actually at a café. A café where you can eat lunch – different menus are offered at noon throughout the week, and you can order a big brunch on Sundays.

The target audience are the young working folks of the neighborhood bordering the 18th and the 9th arrondissement. The aim is to keep them there for as long as possible, because at dusk the Bar à Bulles transforms into a proper bar with cocktails and tapas. Try the Mojito Moulin Rouge (rum, champagne, absinthe, hibiscus tea, and mint). But ssshhh – do not tell anybody about the place!

Address 90 Boulevard de Clichy, 75018 Paris, +33 (0)1 53 41 88 90 | **Getting there** Metro to Blanche (Line 2) | **Hours** Wed–Sat noon–midnight; Sun noon–10pm | **Tip** Don't panic! The nearby Dirty Dick is no longer a *bar à hôtesses*, or the kind of place meant for those looking for a little more than a drink. Today, it is one of the hip new spots in SoPi (South Pigalle). And since we're in the tropics, the bar's cocktails are served in tiki mugs inspired by Easter Island, or glasses in the shape of seashells or coconuts… (10 Rue Frochot, 9th arrondissement, Sun–Sat 6pm–2am).

11 Baton Rouge

Just like on the bayou...

Tired of the stiff vibe of your everyday cocktail bar? Looking for a good drink mixed by one of the best bartenders in the French capital? Then head to the southern end of Pigalle, a neighborhood in the middle of a renaissance that simply does not stop dishing out new surprises. This one is the Baton Rouge, a new bar by Joseph Biolatto and Julien Escot that instantly transports you to Louisiana. The two partners in crime, both internationally recognized for their cocktails, serve up recipes as surprising as they are flavorful, all in an ambiance murmuring with touches of creole identity and voodoo... Culture shock guaranteed! Behind the wrought iron gates that make the establishment so discreet, the bayou is not far.

Baton Rouge (or *Bâton-Rouge* in French) is the capital of Louisiana, a mixing pot of Caribbean, Cajun, and American Indian cultures. These multiple influences have always inspired bartenders, and the art of the cocktail has long blossomed in Louisiana. Old classics such as the Sazerac were created there, and the reputation of Louisiana rum lives up to its name. After all, America's oldest distillery is in New Orleans.

In 1937, Stanley Clisby Arthur wrote *Famous New Orleans Drinks and how to Mix'em*. The book traces the years following the end of prohibition in America, and these are the recipes that inspired the menu at Baton Rouge. Our favorite? The Hurricane, a mixture of three types of rum, lemon juice and passion fruit syrup. But that is just a suggestion, and the menu has more than twenty cocktails with or without alcohol. You're sure to find your own! Not to mention that you're allowed – encouraged, even – to throw your peanut shells on the floor! Once the shock abates, you will be surprised how quickly you get used to it. In terms of snacks, ribs are the house special, and they are finger lickin' good. Without a doubt, the best in Paris.

Address 62 Rue Notre-Dame-de-Lorette, 75009 Paris, +33 (0)1 6 52 90 36 42, www.batonrouge.paris.fr | Getting there Metro to Pigalle (Lines 2 and 12) | Hours Mon–Sat 6pm–2am | Tip When the French explorer Pierre Le Moyne d'Iberville discovered the region in 1699, he described red sticks or *bâtons rouges* – Cyprus trunks used as sacrificial poles that were topped with animal heads and coated in blood, which marked the territorial limits of the Houmas and Bayougoulas tribes – from which came the name of the American city. But luckily, no traces of that here! Though you will find some strange sticks in the interior…

12 Belushi's Canal

Rock 'n' roll urinals

The urinals at Belushi's café, adjacent to the St Christopher's Canal youth hostel, are sure to bring back memories to certain generations of rockers. Inspired by the famous Rolling Stones "Tongue and Lips" logo from the 1971 Sticky Fingers album, these gaping red lips are not those of an angry feminist on a social media rant, but Mick Jagger's own. According to the bar's management, these enticing urinals were purchased in China and eventually made their way into the bar bathroom. You can find the same urinals at the Belushi's in Shepherd's Bush, London.

Everyone comes to Belushi's to see the toilets, including celebrities, athletes, and pop stars, not to mention locals and dusty backpackers from around the world. In any case, these urinals fit right into the vibe of the pub, with its walls covered in posters of rockers, and with its packed program of events, live concerts, and sports broadcasts. During the day, have a drink out on the terrace where you can literally dip your feet in the waters of the canal. It is a good spot for watching the lift bridge from the rue de Crimée, that has been positioned at the entry of the Canal de L'Ourcq since 1885 – the only example of its kind in Paris.

For once, lift your nose up from your smartphone! It would be a pity to miss the show. With its old wheels activating the lifting system to let boats pass underneath, this bridge with its little adjacent walkway is always crowded with tourists trying to follow the footsteps of illustrious photographers like Doisneau, Brassaï, and Atget!

You'd think you were in Amsterdam – an atmosphere reinforced on the bank across the river where you can go to have a pint at the PBC (Panama Brewing Company) brasserie – with its long wooden tables and old-fashioned glistening kegs, all installed in this former firemen's barracks-turned-university dormitory.

Address 159 Rue de Crimée, 75019 Paris | Getting there Metro to Riquet (Line 7) | Tip The bar belongs to St Christopher's Inns, part of a chain of contemporary youth hostels, in a beautiful modern building with a view onto the Bassin de la Villette. There's also a nightclub and sauna.

13__Belvedere of Willy Ronis

When art rises up

Overlooking the park of the same name, the Belleville Belvedere offers an unobstructed view of the capital. It is dedicated to the artists of the neighborhood, including the urban artist Julien "Seth" Malland, whose frescoes adorn it. The park was recently renamed for Willy Ronis, the famous photographer who lived in the 20th arrondissement until his death in 2009. He left behind a trove of incredible black and white photographs taken in the 50s of the old neighborhoods of Belleville and Ménilmontant.

Another name recalled by this promontory is that of Antoine Grumbach, the urbanist architect who constructed it on the roof of the Maison de l'Air in the 90s. Appointed to rehabilitate the area, he chose to preserve its original structure, its little streets and back alleys, its artisan ateliers and its small businesses – everything that gives the neighborhood its charm. It is easy to imagine Belleville as 19th-century countryside with mills, outdoor dancehalls (*les guingettes*), and farms among the vineyards and fields.

Belleville Park was inaugurated on this hill in 1988. If you enter through the bottom, from rue Julien-Lacrois, you have to climb a ways up to earn the view. But it is true, as the inscriptions say, that the panorama is unique. On a clear day, the Eiffel and Montparnasse towers, even the Défense towers, can be seen with the help of binoculars.

Four compass chairs made by the artist Dara Renaud offer quirky seats where weary walkers can rest up a bit. Try the one at the far right, you will see why! At the back, at the intersection of rue des Envierges and rue du Transvaal, there's a charming square with bistro tables – a place to repose between the sky and the earth. The Belvedere is especially lively each year from the beginning of May to the end of September, when it hosts a festival of creators and artists of the neighborhood.

Address 27 Rue Piat, 75020 Paris | Getting there Metro to Pyrénées (Line 11) or Belleville (Lines 2 and 11) | Hours Wed & Sat 1pm–5pm (Oct–Mar), 1:30pm–5:30pm (Apr–Sep) | Tip Under the Belvedere, the Maison de l'Air offers updates on air quality in Paris, with measurements on the Airparif network and Météosat satellite images.

14_ The Bigot Building
Façades of glazed ceramic

You think you have seen all the different façades Paris's apartment buildings have to offer? Sure, you might know the one at 31 Rue Campagne-Première, but have you ever gone through the Passage d'Enfer (just up a bit on the same street) to check out number 25? The two façades should be seen together, in fact, like twin sisters. The first is majestic, the second more discreet, but they are both charming enough to deserve your extended attention.

These two buildings, both of which house artist ateliers, were constructed in 1911 by the architect André Arfvidson, and they won him an award at the *concours des façades de la Ville de Paris*, the city's famous façade competition. The prize was well earned: Arfvidson took a huge risk in collaborating with Alexandre Bigot, the artist known for his work in glazed ceramic. The beige-brown plant-motif tiles he designed for the two buildings have a unique beauty and manage to highlight all the different openings of the building – from the full-length windows facing the street on number 31, to the simple bow windows opening onto the back alley of the lesser known number 25.

If the décor is pure art nouveau, the distribution of units inside number 31 is totally modern. In fact, it was the first place in Paris to have two-floor duplex apartments.

The building was luxurious even for the period in which it was built – and do not get any ideas about its initial residents being struggling artists. Even though at the time, Montparnasse was a refuge for all the bohemians fleeing the skyrocketing rents of Montmartre, they definitely could not have afforded the duplex ateliers in this building. Even back then, it was targeted towards bourgeois residents in search of an "artsy" vibe. With one possible exception: the American photographer Man Ray lived here while he was with the famous Kiki de Montparnasse, the famous model of *les Années Folles*.

Address 31 Rue de Campagne-Première, 25 Passage d'Enfer, 75014 Paris | Getting there Metro to Raspail (Lines 4 and 6) | Tip If you are a fan of ceramic tiles in general, check out the stunning façade of the Céraic Hôtel (39 Rue de Wagram, 75017 Paris), another work of Bigot in a style even more marked by the art nouveau aesthetic. The first three floors are covered completely in ceramic.

15 _ The Bois Dormoy

A communal garden

A tiny forest in the middle of Paris? One that grew freely for a mile along the railroad tracks of the 18th arrondissement? You don't believe it? You should.

Leave the always-bustling Rue Max-Domroy, go down a cul-de-sac, la Cité de la Chapelle, and there waiting in plain sight is something Paris could use many more of: a big garden planted with beautiful trees that have been growing without hindrance for twenty years, a corner of greenery in a neighborhood that is cruelly lacking in it. Impressive poplars take up one part of the space, rubbing shoulders with willows and maples, forming a canopy that reaches impressive density in places. The budleja or butterfly bush, which grows very easily in the wild, glimmers with colorful flowers. Along the promenade, you will notice mouthwatering strawberry and raspberry bushes…

The locals have created community gardens here, where they grow cabbages, artichokes, lettuces, and tomatoes, and kids from the nearby school also come to tend. Since 2008, the Association Sauvons le Bois Dormoy, or "Save the Bois Dormoy Association" has sponsored several open houses and events, including artist ateliers, photography exhibitions, picnics, concerts, outdoor cinema, story times for children.

So that solidarity does not become merely a word, ties have been made with other local associations such as Emmaüs, La Table ouverte, which brings together retirees from the Maghreb, and L'Échomusée de la Goutte d'Or, a museum that supports artistic creations inspired by the neighborhood.

One tip: hurry up and go visit this park and talk to the people who run it! For years, the city council has been trying to get rid of it in order to make room for a real estate development project opposed by "Save the Bois Dormoy." Your heart will surely drop at the thought that this special place might disappear forever.

Address Cité de la Chapelle, 75018 Paris, www.boisdormoy.blogspot.fr | Getting there Metro to La Chapelle (Line 2) or Max Dormoy (Line 12) | Hours Sundays from 3pm | Tip Run by Table ouverte, the ICI is a community café in the Goutte d'Or neighborhood (Institut des Cultures d'Islam, 19–23 Rue Léon, Mon–Sat 9am–6pm). On the outdoor patio or inside the colorful main room they serve very good local cuisine.

16 Butte Bergeyre
The village up on a perch

Strolling down the sidewalks of Rue Manin or Avenue Simon-Bolivar, you won't be able to miss the enormous staircases nestled between the tall grey buildings. The view has to be earned, though – you will have to climb over 300 feet up to reach the top of the Butte Bergeyre. But the village up on a perch is a charming little surprise, with its five paved streets. The place is absolutely enchanting with all its villas, each cuter than the next, and their little mini-gardens drooping with wisteria and climbing with rosebushes. The houses were built in the 1930s, at the site of the Bergeyre stadium, named after a star rugby player who died in 1914 at 20 years old. Wander around a bit and when you pass in front of 70 Rue Georges-Lardennois, take a look at the Villa Zilveli: an incredible house on stilts erected in 1933 by the Austrian architect Jean Welz. You will notice the façade under the Virginia creeper. You will arrive very quickly to the viewpoint, the highest spot on the hill, on top of a few acres of vineyards called the Clos des Chaufourniers, which produces 100 bottles of wine annually of mostly Chardonnay and Pinot Noir grapes. Just underneath, the street of the same name recalls the past of workers in the nearby limekilns, where they made blocks of plaster when the Buttes-Chaumont hills were quarries.

On the west side, at the top of the hill, you will end up at a bench looking out over an extraordinary view spotlighting the Sacré-Cœur of Montmartre. To the left you will spot the two rival towers, Eiffel and Montparnasse. Maybe you will stay there to reflect on the city and its gems – unless you're interrupted by the joyful rumblings coming from the communal gardens or a neighborhood picnic. It is a total block party vibe: kids playing in a closed-off area, with six beehives installed in 2013 that produce 375 pounds of honey.

Address Access via stairs at 21 Rue Manin, 54 Avenue Simon-Bolivar and Rue Michel-Tagrine | **Getting there** Metro to Bolivar or Buttes Chaumont (Line 7bis) | **Tip** Jean-Chalres Alphand, the chief engineer of Haussman, inaugurated the Buttes-Chaumont Park on May 1, 1867: 60 acres of lawn with a lake, a 100-foot-high waterfall, a grotto, and the temple of Sibylle.

17__Butte du Chapeau-Rouge Park

A call to peace

Gypsum is everywhere in Paris – it is the material used on all those prototypically Parisian buildings with white plaster façades. The Parc de la Butte du Chapeau-Rouge rests on a vast grid of quarries from which the gypsum was extracted. This nearly 12-hectare park is named for a former *guingette* dance hall of the Pré-Saint-Gervais.

On Sunday, May 25, 1913, from atop this hillock, the socialist Jean Jaurès addressed a crowd of 150,000 people to denounce both the carnage of the war and military draft, which had been extended to three years of service. Maybe you've seen the famous photo of Jaurès haranguing his supporters with a bowler hat atop his head – it was taken right here! The gathering had been banned from taking place at the Père-Lachaise cemetery, where every May 25 people went to pay homage to those who died in the Paris Commune. So Jaurès opted for this hillock that at the time was part of the town of Pré-Saint-Gervais.

Today the red flags are gone, but the panoramic view is still there, stretching all the way to the peripheral towns on the east of Paris – Le Pré-Saint-Gervais, Pantin, Les Lilas, and Bobigny. Neighborhood residents come to hang out on the grass or enjoy the sculpture by the Luxembourger artist Bert Theis, which can be found in the alley above the imposing fountain: two big wooden benches painted white, symbolizing peace – a reference to the 1913 speech. The sculpture was built by carpentry students from the apprenticeship program in Noisy-le-Grand.

The trees in the park are also an attraction: Bohemian olives, weeping pagodas, the ginkgo biloba – in French, the *arbre aux quarante écus*, or the "40-écus tree," so-called because that was the price paid for it by its first owner. Originally from the Far East, this very ancient tree has fan-shaped leaves and produces almonds you can eat.

Address 5 Avenue Debidour, access from Boulevard d'Algérie, 75019 Paris | **Getting there** Metro to Pré-Saint-Gervais (Line 7bis) or tram to Hôpital Robert Debré (Line T3b) | **Tip** The place is taking off! Every year, from the end of August through the beginning of September, the park welcomes the Silhouette festival, which shows films for the young and old alike, along with outdoor concerts for everyone! (www.association-silhouette.com)

18__ Café A

For the uber-hip

To get to Café A, situated between the Gare de l'Est and the Canal Saint-Martin, you have to know the spot, because the entry gate and the exterior archways do not hint at all at what's to come. Inside is a superb room, followed by a big courtyard planted with hundred-year-old trees and protected from the street by a city wall.

Backed by Henri IV, the order of the Récollets was established in this area outside the walls of Paris. This monastery, which at one point had more than 200 monks, was established at this site in 1619. Sacked during the Revolution, it became a hospice and then a military hospital, where a famous doctor named de Villeman discovered that tuberculosis was contagious.

When the hospital was evacuated in 1971, an architecture school set up shop in the part of the building that was saved. Twenty years later, a collective of artists, "Les anges des Récollets," made its quarters there. But in 1992, a fire damaged the buildings, and after that their future became uncertain. There was even talk of destroying them. Without the mobilization of a collective of artists and architects, along with the local residents, no one would be there today sipping coffee and listening to music.

Which just goes to show how far it has come! Today, it houses the Maison de l'architecture, a residency of researchers and artists from around the whole world, and the regional board of architects.

Not to mention the famous Café A. Supported by tall metal beams, the loft-like room is decorated by young Parisian artists, who can use all the support they can get. On weekends there are live concerts, performance art shows, and movie-concerts. The clientele is mostly hipsters who come to drink (organic) wine and dip into cheese or charcuterie platters while elbowing their way for a spot at the bar. For those who prefer peace and quiet, go visit in the afternoon and read in a chaise longue in the courtyard.

Address 148 Rue du Faubourg-Saint-Martin, 75010 Paris, +33 (0)9 81 29 83 38 | Getting there Metro to Gare de l'Est (Lines 4, 5, and 7) | Hours May–Sep Sat & Sun 10am–2am; Oct–Apr Tue–Sat 10am–2am | Tip If you come to Café A during the week, cross the canal afterwards to take a peek at the courtyard of the Hôpital Saint-Louis, paved in brick and stone dating back to Henri IV. The king commissioned this royal hospital to fight the ravages of the epidemics of the era. The building was conceived as a place that could be contained from the rest of the city (2 Place du Docteur-Alfred-Fournier).

19___ Café des Chats

The stress-relieving coffee break

"I like cats! Let's go!" my son said to me when I told him about the Café des Chats. In our house, cats are as sacred as in Ancient Egypt! But it is Japanese culture being paid homage by Margaux Gandelon, the creator of this tea-salon-slash-restaurant. The anti-stress effect of felines on city-dwellers has been used in bars since 2004. In Paris, Gandelon opened the first cat-café in 2013 in the Marais, followed by another in the Bastille (9 Rue Sedaine, 11th arrondissement).

Reservations are required to dine in the company of these four-legged lodgers. Once inside, you have to rub some disinfectant on your hands and respect the rules: do not wake a sleeping cat, do not pick them up, and above all stay Zen.

All of the kitties were rescued from animal shelters, and here they get the best of care. Everything is done to keep them in harmony: each kitty has its own dish and its own favorite spot. Beatrice, an executive at a stressful job, comes here often. "I have a cat at home, but I miss him during the day, so I come here. It is really therapeutic. You see the red and white one? That is Simba, the explorer. He likes to nestle in people's bags and strollers. Careful not to leave with him! That one is Oréa. When she falls asleep on my knees, I cannot even leave!"

All christened with carefully chosen names, the cats have their photos and biographies displayed on the walls, a good way to familiarize yourself with them. You learn that Salem, a black cat with funny spots who was found in the hallway of an apartment building and who is quite at ease with humans, always goes for the cushiest armchairs. Khaleesi, a Siamese cross, welcomes clients like a geisha as they enter. There's also Ringo, Chloé, Idylle… (I don't want anyone to feel left out, but I cannot name all of them!) As for Zan, the all-black newest little guy, he is a naughty little thing.

Address 9 Rue Sedaine, 75011 Paris, contact@lecafedeschats.fr | **Getting there** Metro to Breguet-Sabin (Line 5) | **Hours** Mon–Fri noon–10:30pm; Sat & Sun noon–11pm | **Tip** The Boulevard Richard-Lenoir covers the Canal Saint-Martin, which opens up further north, but the two squares make for a very agreeable promenade with fountains, games of boules, and play areas for children.

20_ The Canal House
The bright life

One sunny day, my friend Pierrina takes me to the *Pavillon des Canaux*, or canal house. This old home to mariners, renovated from floor to ceiling by the artsy Sinny & Ooko agency, offers an exceptional terrace where you can practically taste the sea breeze! We're looking out onto a direct view of the basin where children are splashing around in their kayaks. Getting out is sure to finish with a capsizing or two… Sure enough – there goes a little blond boy into the water! Luckily the instructor scoops him out quickly.

Reassured, we look up to admire the cheery printed-paper decorating the façade and we go inside. And there, we're totally blown away. It is stunning. Bright colors everywhere: on the walls, on the furniture – mostly salvaged or thrifted, but all quite pretty – on the tiles, even on the floorboards of the staircase. The whole interior puts you in a good mood.

On the ground floor, a restaurant-bar offers tempting *gateaux maison*, along with a menu of small plates at modest prices. A corner salon lets you sit down at a table to recharge or do some work. In between mealtimes, the place is meant to be a workspace where you can stay and connect to Wi-Fi.

On the second floor, the surprises keep coming. A delicious smell first leads us to a little gem of a kitchen where a young *pâtissière* reigns over the pastries. The kitchen leads into a salon painted blue with a chimney; that is next to a pink bedroom and a bathroom where the bathtub is a banquette! The downstairs bathroom is done up as a *salon de voyance*, or a clairvoyant's salon. It is a place for everyone, whether you live in the neighborhood or not, and they offer all sorts of fun activities: decorating workshops, cooking classes, life-coaching sessions, tastings, meditation classes, a hair salon, coffee meet-ups for parents, and a crafts workshop for kids called the *atelier La Grande Bricole*.

Address 39 Quai de la Laoire, 75019 Paris, +33 (0)1 73 71 82 90, www.pavillondescanaux.com | **Getting there** Metro to Laumière (Line 5) or Riquet (Line 7) | **Hours** Mon–Wed 10am–midnight; Thu–Sat 10am–1am; Sun 10am–10pm | **Tip** Just next door, Parisians can learn to row in crew boats, canoes, or kayaks at the Base Nautique. (Adults: Sat (except in bad weather) 9am–noon and 2pm–5pm; 12- to 17-year-olds: Wed and camps during school vacations; +33 (0)1 42 76 30 00).

21__ The Chapal Factory

A new skin for a former rabbit fur factory

There's not much left of Montreuil's industrial past, which once counted up to 755 factories, but a few vestiges do remain. Among the most spectacular is the Chapal factory, or the *Usine Chapal*, which closed its doors in 1968, and which was the biggest fur brand in Europe specializing in rabbit skins.

Descended from a long line of fur trappers from La Creuse, Marien Chapal came to Montreuil in 1857 to establish his tannery. It was the beginning of a long family saga. In 1882, the Chapals opened a factory in Brooklyn, with other locations following soon thereafter in Crocq (in La Creuse), Lagny-sur-Marne, and elsewhere in France. Chapal made a name for itself, and ultimately became a veritable multinational company that absorbed its competition. In 1913, the brand began making jackets and suits for the air force, and in 1934, they introduced their famous *bombardier*, the iconic leather bomber jacket still sought-after today.

Many big artists visited the factory in Montreuil. The filmmaker and illusionist Georges Méliès, who had his studios nearby, even made a documentary there. During its heyday, the factory employed about 2,000 people. But it ended up being a victim of the factory strikes and occupations of 1968 and had to shut down. Parts of the space were demolished, while the rest served as a warehouse until 1990. The Chapal brand still exists today, however, run by Jean-François Bardinon, a 6th-generation heir of the family company. It now specializes in high-end pieces and leatherwork for automobiles.

To save this bit piece of industrial heritage, Bardinon invited about 60 artists to come make their studios in the building, and the place is now a vibrant artistic center. It is part of what makes Montreuil a cultural hotspot that is really having a moment. It is a bit like the Brooklyn of Paris, with more than 800 artists living and working there.

Address 2 Rue Marcelin-Berthelot, 93100 Montreuil | **Getting there** Metro to Croix de Chevaux (Line 9) | **Hours** Visits to the artists' ateliers during open houses, which start the second or third weekend in October | **Tip** The industrial heritage of the city, which includes the former Pernod factory at 87 Rue de Paris, can be explored with the guided city tours arranged by the Tourism Office of Montreuil. (www.montreuiltourisme.fr, +33 (0)1 41 58 14 09)

22 — Château Rothschild
The poetry of ruins

Its silhouette dominates the splendid Edmond-de-Rothschild Park, but the Sunday strollers barely notice it as they frolic on the vast lawns leading to the lake and the Japanese garden. This castle in ruins is far from the building that the young banker James de Rothschild built between 1851 and 1861.

A Louis XIV-style construction, the castle's façades boasted marble columns, balconies, and a large wall of glass windows. One of the salons was hung with works by François Boucher and the walls of the large dining room were covered in Cordoue leather. The castle enjoyed its glory days under Napoleon III, when the Rothschild family welcomed all the *grands hommes* and artists of the period.

During World War II, Nazis sacked the castle before American troops looted its contents. The Rothschild family hasn't lived there since. But in 1951, Miriam-Alexandrine de Rothschild succeeded in getting it landmarked. In 1969, 15 acres of the estate were annexed for the new Ambroise-Paré hospital and in 1974, the estate was further amputated for the A13 junction of the belt highway. Since then, the Rothschild castle has been little more than a shadow, if an inspiring one. Marguerite Duras filmed *India Song* there in 1975, and then *Son nom de Venise dans Calcutta désert* in 1976. In both works, you can spot a few recognizable images of the building, like the famous horseshoe staircase descending onto the Boulogne Park, or the succession of majestically filmed rooms.

The last owner from the Rothschild family was the baron Edmond, who gave the last 37 acres to the park in the city of Boulogne for the symbolic price of one franc.

In 1986, the castle was bought by a sheikh – the son-in-law of the king of Saudi Arabia. Squatted, tagged with graffiti, twice burnt down, and overgrown with bramble, the castle has fallen back asleep while awaiting better days.

Address Parc de Boulogne – Edmond-de-Rothschild, 3 Rue des Victoires, at the corner of Rue de l'Abreuvoir and Rue Saint-Denis, 92100 Boulogne-Billancourt | Getting there Metro to Boulogne – Jean-Jaurès (Line 10) followed by a free minibus | Tip At the entry to the park, the Pavillon Buchillot (a hot spot of the 18th century) houses the Musée Paul-Belmondo (14 Rue de l'Abreuvoir, Tue – Fri 2pm – 6pm; Sat & Sun 11am – 6pm except holidays).

23 Chemin des Vignes

Issy, the place to be

Behind the new constructions popping up along the Seine, in Issy-les-Moulineaux, there's a secret address worth discovering. A large vaulted doorway hides an incredible labyrinth of wine cellars, run by the Legrand family, whose story is a veritable saga.

In 1912, two twin brothers, Pierre and Alexandre Legrand, opened a grocery store in the Corentin Celton neighborhood of Issy-les-Moulineaux. After the war, when the shop had become too small, they decided to open an identical outpost in Paris on Rue de la Banque. When Alexandre retired, only the Paris shop, which sold wines and fine groceries, stayed open. But the story of the family was not finished. In 1975, Lucien, the son of Pierre, bought some quarries in Issy in an area called Le Chemin des Vignes – a portentous name. And so the descendants of these two pioneering twins took over the family business, which now includes a winery, a boutique and a restaurant.

Once upon a time, the Paris Basin was home to the biggest vineyard of France, as cultivating grapes outside the city limits allowed certain taxes to be avoided. In Issy, grapevines represented three quarters of the cultivated lands. At the Chemin des Vignes, the vineyard is situated just above the wine cellar. The 400 or so vines are a mix of chardonnay and pinot, which thrive under maximum sunlight. Harvested by ten-year-olds from a nearby school, the wine is then vinified in the 250-year-old cellars over five floors of caves carefully maintained at a constant temperature of 59 degrees Fahrenheit. The tour is full of surprises, like the several works by contemporary artists inspired by the vineyard – a lovely way of showcasing emerging talents. The visit to the cellars is by appointment and includes tastings. At the dinners, a wine producer presents the best bottles from the region, and you can also rent space to organize private parties!

Address 113 Avenue de Verdun, 92130 Issy-les-Moulineaux, +33 (0)1 46 38 11 66, www.chemindesvignes.net | Getting there RER to Issy (Line 3) | Tip To prolong your pleasure, hop on over to Issy Guingete, just above the cellars, where Mathieu Legrand prepares dishes from the vegetable garden with pigs raised on the farm or lamb from Lozère cooked for seven hours. It will melt in your mouth, guaranteed! (reservations: +33 (0)1 46 62 04 27).

24 Chemin du Montparnasse

Chasing after les Années Folles

Just under the Tour Montparnasse and on the right, this bucolic enclave of artists is nothing short of miraculous! Constructed with recuperated materials from the Universal Exposition of 1900, this still intact oasis of calm and greenery glimmers with the bohemian spirit of les Années Folles. All of the artistic avant-garde of the École de Paris could be found there during the 1920s.

Today the ateliers, whose crooked structures remain standing in spite of their age, are occupied by a new generation of artists. You can spot their works through the wisteria and creeper-covered front windows. Two of the largest ateliers are open to the public.

To the left, you will find the Villa Vassilief, named for the Russian artist Marie Vassilieff (1884–1957), who came to study painting in Paris under Matisse before setting up her own art school here in 1921. It quickly became a hangout for artists like Braque, Juan Gris, Matisse, Modigliani, Fernand Léger, Picasso, Soutine, and Zadkine, along with literary figures and musicians including Apollinaire, Cocteau, and Satie.

During the war, in 1915, the artist opened a cafeteria where she offered a full meal with wine to artists in need, for the price of a few centimes. The place was also known for its wild parties that raged late into the night. From 1998 to 2013, the atelier of Marie Vassilieff was home to the Musée de Montparnasse. Now it is a cultural space dedicated to visual arts, with residencies for artists and researchers.

A bit farther, at the end of the cul-de-sac, there is another quirky spot called l'Espace Krajcberg, named for the Polish-born Brazilian sculptor and photographer Frans Kracjberg. Born in 1921, he dedicated his life and art to ecological causes, and fought against deforestation in the Amazon. Be sure to check out his amazing works made of burnt tree trunks and roots.

Address 21 Avenue du Maine, 75015 Paris | **Getting there** Metro to Montparnasse-Bienvenue (Lines 4, 6, 12, and 13) or Falguière (Line 12) | **Hours** Villa Marie Vassilieff, Tue–Sat 11am–7pm; Espace Krajcberg, every day (except Mon) 2pm–6pm | **Tip** The mythical La Coupole brasserie, an historical monument dating from 1927 and a gem of art deco style, is covered in frescoes painted by the artists of Montparnasse. On one of the room's columns, Marie Vassilieff completed the portrait of the author Georges Duhamel. (102 Boulevard du Montparnasse, 75014 Paris, +33 (0)1 43 20 14 20, Mon–Fri 8am–11pm; Sat, Sun & holidays 8am–midnight, www.lacoupole-paris.com/fr)

25 _ The Chen Zhen Fountain
Water's symbolic path

It is called the *Fontaine de l'eau émergente*, or the Fountain of
Emerging Water. This headless dragon, whose body emerges from
the underground water production plant of Austerlitz and weaves
through the paving stones, is the last piece designed by the French-
Chinese artist Chen Zhen (1955–2000). His wife, Xu Min, also
an artist, completed it eight years after his death. The dragon's path
pays homage to the role water has played in this site for over three
centuries. The statue peeks out of the sidewalk like a dragon partly
submerged in a river, and is oriented along a northwest-southwest
axis, between the Seine (the yin) and the sun (the yang). This
placement of the dragon corresponds to the precepts of Ancient
Chinese wisdom.

The statue symbolizes not only the role of water in the history
of Paris, but also the encounter between the artist's two cultural
identities. The glass-and-steel structure is fitted with thousands of
jets that send high-pressure water through the transparent tubes –
you can see the water running through the dragon's transparent body.
The recirculated water comes from a special treatment unit located in
the basement of the Austerlitz plant. In winter, like most fountains in
Paris, it is turned off to avoid freezing, but at nightfall, the creature is
lit up in bright colors thanks to a variable lighting system controlled
by a timer.

In 2015, on the *Journées du patrimoine* national holiday, the
Austerlitz plant (which was built on this historic site) opened its
doors to reveal its secrets to the public. Since 1994, the plant has been
used as a water treatment center, preparing water from the Seine to
be dispersed throughout the city to quench the thirst of its parks and
green spaces. Nicknamed "the underground Beaubourg," it is made
up of an impressive network of pipes 65 feet deep – far below the
level of the river.

Address Place Augusta-Holmes, 75013 Paris | Getting there Metro to Quai de la Gare (Line 6) | Tip Follow the Seine to Les Docks – Cité de la Mode et du Design and hang out at the Moon Roof terrace, a restaurant and lounge bar with a unique view of the Seine (www.citemodedesign.fr, 34 Quai d'Austerlitz).

26__The Chocolate Museum
The history of hot chocolate

Since 2010, Paris has boasted one museum not quite like the rest. You will leave not only with your soul enriched with new knowledge, but also with your taste buds tingling with the taste of chocolate. Think you can resist a visit?

Don't fall for the austerity of the façade – this museum is full of surprises and will make the whole family happy. It traces the history of chocolate from the Americas to Europe, thanks to the collection of the Belgian entrepreneur Eddy Van Belle, a longtime fan of this sweet subject, who previously founded an identical museum in Bruges in Belgium.

The history of chocolate starts in the Pre-Columbian Americas, where the Mayans used cocoa in all sorts of important roles: the beans served as currency, and the drink they made from it was considered sacred, reserved for royalty and nobles. In Mayan culture, it was made by grinding the cocoa beans with corn kernels into a ball of paste. They'd break off a small portion according to need, which was then diluted with boiling water and spiced to taste. In the 16th century, the Spanish brought the beans back to the Old World where they started being mixed with sugar and milk, becoming the chocolate drink we know and love today. Anne of Austria, the royal daughter of Spain, was the first person to serve hot chocolate in the French court, at her marriage to Louis XIII in 1615.

By the 17th century, it had become all the rage among French high society, who guzzled it down without necessarily digesting it very well: these were the days before skim milk, and so it was very heavy. But the trend was there, and trends had to be followed – especially in the chicest salons of Paris! In the museum, try to find the star of the collection: the famous "tasse-moustache" cup. It is proof of the ingenuity of mustached society: the upper part let men drink their hot chocolate without sullying their 'tache.

Address 28 Boulevard de Bonne-Nouvelle, 75010 Paris, +33 (0)1 42 29 68 60,
www.museeduchocolat.fr | Getting there Metro to Bonne Nouvelle (Lines 8 and 9) |
Hours Every day 10am–6pm (last entry at 5pm) | Tip Purists will want to try out the
Aztec hot chocolate: it is the closest to the ancient recipe. But careful – it is spicy! Chili
pepper is the main ingredient after chocolate.

27 ─ Ciné 13 Theater

A nice family history

Ciné 13 was started by Claude Lelouch, but it is also run by his daughter Salomé, the noble heir of a long line of artists. Bathed in cinema and theater since childhood, she's dabbled in acting too: she was in the 1994 film *Quand j'avais cinq ans, je m'ai tué*, along with several other features directed by her father. It has been over ten years since she jumped into the adventure of Ciné 13 Théâtre, a place that combines stage shows, film programming, cinema-concerts, and exhibitions.

Ciné 13 was built by her father Claude as the location to film his 1983 feature *Edith et Marcel*, with the main room decked out in 1920s décor. Évelyne Bouix, Salomé's mother, played Édith Piaf alongside Marcel Cerdan Junior in the role of his own father, the famous boxer. For years, Claude Lelouch debuted all his films at Ciné 13, before handing over distribution to his sister Martine. He likes to keep it all in the family.

Located in the heart of Montmartre, practically leaning on the Moulin de la Galette, the Ciné 13 sits at the tip-top of the very chic avenue Junot, lined with splendid houses, many of which match the art deco style of the theater. It has an intimate and timeless feel that is quite charming, especially on the little balcony on the second floor. In the first rows of the theater, Salomé Lelouch has kept up the wide red couches from the early days of Ciné 13. Its programming gives star billing to original creations. There are some for children – *Antoinette, the Wise Hen*, a mini-opera in French and in English, for example. For adults, there are romantic comedies and epics – for example *2 bras 2 jambes*, the story of a 20-month trek to Asia in which Françoise Dasque brings to life the characters she met along the way. The audience keeps coming back – they are loyal to this place that seems to come straight out of the old village of Montmartre.

Address 1 Avenue Junot, 75018 Paris, +33 (0)1 42 54 15 12, www.cine13-theatre.com |
Getting there Metro to Abbesses or Lamarck – Caulaincourt (Line 12) | **Tip** At Ciné 13 there is a wine bar where you can keep having fun after the show, or even eat a bite before – they offer cheese platters of various sizes.

28__ Cité du Cinéma

Hollywood-sur-Seine

No, I did not run into Natalie Portman filming *Jackie*. But it was a sort of homecoming for the star featured at the age of 13 by Luc Besson in his 1993 film *Léon*, which was filmed right here in what was once an electrical power plant. And in this same spot, the director realized his project "Hollywood-sur-Seine du 9-3" after several years of preparation.

Opened in September 2012, the Cité du Cinéma brings together a production house, nine studios, a projection room, and two film schools, l'École Nationale Supérieure Louis-Lumière and l'École de la Cité. The second school is tuition-free and accessible to everyone, with no prerequisites except for a solid ambition. Besson himself had humble beginnings in the "7th art," working as a simple stagehand at the age of 17 years old.

The architecture of the Nef, the main building, is striking. Magnificently renovated in art deco style, it is stunning due to its length – over 700 feet – and because of its high windows encased in metal. Built in 1906, it used to be the electrical plant that powered the Paris Metro. Right in the middle sits the old turbine, now painted in technicolor hues. At the end, the overhead cranes have stuck around. A few souvenirs from movies filmed here are exhibited: Michel Vaillant's car, Korben Dallas' taxi from the *Fifth Element*, and many other relics of cinema's most vibrant moments.

From our guide Anne-Sophie, I discovered lots of things about filming. I learned that the costumes from *Les Aventures extraordinaires d'Adèle Blanc-Sec* were made to measure from four samples for Louise Bourgoin. I saw the famous staircase from the film *Léon*. I went into studio 5, the biggest at 21,000 square feet and over 50 feet tall, and whose floor covers a pit 10 feet deep. I even met a real director who teaches at l'École de la Cité, Rachid Dhibou. A fascinating place!

Address 20 Rue Ampère, 93200 Saint-Denis | Getting there Metro to Carrefour Pleyel (Line 13) | Hours Visits by reservation through Cultival (www.cultival.fr) | Tip Centre de Saint-Denis is not far – go visit the basilica at 1 Rue de la Légion-d'Honneur. It is a masterpiece of gothic art, where you can find the tombs of the kings of France.

29___Le Clown Bar

Life's a three-ring circus

What kid does not love the circus? I sure did. I was always thrilled when a circus company debarked in my little hometown: the big top in bright red, the roar of a lion – because there's always a lion – the clowns, and the trapeze artists I wanted to imitate. Just thinking about those memories fills me with joy. But there's no need for the real deal. Just head to the Clown Bar, which has become a hot restaurant in the 11th arrondissement. Its décor itself is worth the trek. On the ceiling, a clown, holding an umbrella over a man in a frock coat, peers down at the 21st-century clients with a ruthless look on his face. Don't worry, he cannot come out and get you – he is stuck behind glass.

On a frieze above the bar called *La Grande Parade des clowns* (The big clown parade), the décor itself puts on a show. The painted clowns jump, dance, and turn acrobatic tricks before a shadowy crowd in the background. This fantastic decorative frieze was made by the architect Jean-Baptiste Memery in the 1920s and was likely mounted by the artist himself. Consisting of panels of ceramic, the frieze was made by the Sarreguemines factory in Moselle. Threatened with demolition in 1987, it was thankfully landmarked in 1995 as an historical monument. Since 1902, when it first opened, the Clown Bar has welcomed all the artists who have appeared in the Cirque d'Hiver. This beautiful building, with its Greek-inspired décor, is just a stone's throw away. Constructed over eight months in 1852 by Jacques Ignace Hittorff, the Cirque d'Hiver has since been magnificently restored and is still open today.

You can go see a show there before testing out the food at Clown Bar, which is currently under the direction of the Japanese chef Atsumi Sota, a real magician of flavors. He designs his menu according to his inspiration, with dishes that are just as pleasing to the eye as they are to the palate.

Address 114 Rue Amelot, 75011 Paris, +33 (0)1 43 55 87 35 | Getting there Metro to Filles du Calvaire (Line 8) | Hours Wed–Sun 8am–10:30pm; closed Dec 24–Jan 6 | Tip To stay in the circus mood, take a tour of La Vache acrobate, on the same street, where you will be welcomed like an old friend. And be sure to try their Charolais cheeseburger – an acrobatic burger topped with delicious Comté cheese! (La Vache Acrobate, 77 Rue Amelot, 75011 Paris, +33 (0)1 47 00 49 42)

30 Les Combattants de la Nueve Garden

In honor of Spanish heroes

If you know French History, you will know about the soldiers of La Nueve, a regiment of France's Second Armored Division during World War II that was headed by General Leclerc. The men of La Nueve were the first to enter Paris and make it into the Hôtel de Ville on the night of August 24, 1944. Their battalion was nicknamed La Nueve, or "nine" in Spanish, because 90% of it was made up of Spanish Republicans. Their lieutenant Amado Granell was the first officer of the French forces to be received by the *Conseil national de la Résistance*.

On June 3, 2015, the heroic survivors of La Nueve were honored in Paris with a ceremony at the Hôtel de Ville, where a little garden was renamed the Jardin des Combattants de la Nueve by Anne Hidalgo, the mayor of Paris. King Felipe VI of Spain and his wife Letizia were also there to unveil the new plaque commemorating the regiment. It is probably the first time in history the king had to trek all the way to France to pay homage to the people of his own country!

This little garden was in fact once the site of a small miracle: during the fire at the Hôtel de Ville on May 24, 1871, its trees managed to escape the flames. It is a long and narrow stretch alongside the Hôtel's south façade, mostly lawn framed in gorgeous beds of roses. During the week, its playground is filled with toddlers from the nearby nursery school. The city council also installed a henhouse for children, so that tiny Parisians can learn how these peaceful birds live and reproduce, and how to take care of them.

On the weekend, this eco-garden is open to the public. Be sure to take a look at the greenhouse, which is filled with fragile plant life. It is a lovely place to walk around, surrounded by whispers of history and the beauty of nature.

Address 2 Place de l'Hôtel-de-Ville – Esplanade de la Libération, 75004 Paris | **Getting there** Metro to Hôtel de Ville (Lines 1 and 11) | **Hours** Sat, Sun, and holidays 9am to sunset | **Tip** In the middle of the garden is the statue of Étienne Marcel, which was inaugurated in 1888 during the reconstruction of the Hôtel de Ville. Marcel is an emblematic figure of the capital: provost to merchants under the reign of Jean II le Bon, in the 14th century, he presided over the municipality.

31 Cour des Bourguignons

The glory days of carpentry

The well-preserved Cour des Bourguignons is one of the last standing relics of the industrial past of Faubourg Saint-Antoine. Since the 16th century, it was the neighborhood of carpenters, who chose to set up shop there because they could easily receive wood shipments transported on the Seine – and because there they were able to avoid regular business taxes. During the 17th century, the furniture became more and more refined – trimmed in golden bronze, porcelain, lacquer, and mother-of-pearl – and so woodworkers and other related artisans began to multiply in the neighborhood.

In the 19th century, there began to be a new type of lodging for craftworkers in what were called artisanal buildings. These units brought together both ateliers and lodgings that shared a central courtyard and a common energy source. The Cour des Bourguignons, built by the wood merchant Charles-Auguste Hollande between 1862 and 1868, is a magnificent example of this situation. The 100-foot-high chimney of the old steam engine, planted right in the middle of the courtyard, is also a rarity. Later, a second courtyard was added, the back of which looks out onto the rue de Charenton.

The whole place was occupied by the Maison Antoine Krieger, founded in 1825, which produced furniture "in styles old and new" and sold at fixed prices. On the walls of the entrance porch, a plaque with partially rubbed-out inscriptions recalls its glorious past. In 1857, Krieger employed over fifty carpenters, sawyers, sculptors and chair-makers. When Krieger started to get annoyed by workers playing hooky to go fish in the Seine or sing in the tunnels of Charonne, he installed a big clock at the entry to keep tabs on them. But the first time the clock rang, it set off a strike – a barricade was even set up in front of the door. Let's just say that after that, the clock stayed quiet.

Address 74 Rue du Faubourg-Saint-Antoine, 75011 Paris | **Getting there** Metro to Bastille (Lines 1, 5 and 8) or Ledru-Rollin (Line 8) | **Tip** The picturesque Marché Couvert Beauveau on Place d'Aligre – open weekdays (except Monday) in the morning and the afternoon, as well as Sunday morning – is one of the oldest covered markets in Paris and among the least expensive. It is also home to the Puces d'Aligre flea market.

32 _ Coudurier Weapons Rooms

A décor worthy of d'Artagnan the musketeer

Once upon a time, fencing was an art and not a sport. There were *salles d'armes*, or weapons rooms, in every neighborhood in Paris, because bourgeois and noblemen alike learned how to handle swords. The Salles d'Armes Coudurier is the oldest in Paris, and still boasts its original décor. It was originally called the Cercle-André-des-Arts before taking the name of Alexandre Coudurier, the young "master of arms" who took it over in 1893. Alexandre was succeeded by his son Maurice, who in turn handed over the reigns in 1973 to Jean-Pierre Pinel de La Taule, who still teaches there today.

Everything has stayed the same, the antique wooden scoreboard, the old rapiers hung from racks, armors, iron masks, and of course the original fencing paths – seven meters long and covered in cork. You'd think you were in a cloak-and-dagger movie! On the wall, a poster reminds us to respect the "Rules established under Louis XIII and Louix XIV and still in use in our days." For the art of *la belle escrime* demands not only strength, balance, flexibility, coordination, but also *bienséance*, or proper decorum.

The weapons room teaches primarily foil, sword, and dry saber fencing, which forces the fencer to announce the touches they receive themself (called "right of way" in English). And careful, cheaters! Even if it is equipped with electric equipment, the honor code rules in this room.

Jean-Pierre Pinel de La Taule instills this sportsmanship and *savoir-vivre* to all the generations who come to his school, even the youngest. During individual lessons, called "au plastron," the novices start with foiling, learning to maneuver with the left hand as well as the right. This is the indispensible foundation for practicing with the sword or the saber, before you can go on to the different coats of arms and start competing. En garde! At the end of my visit, I got a touch!

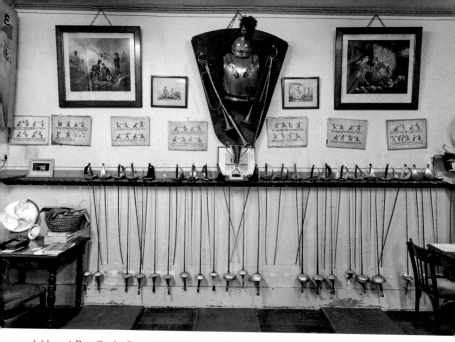

Address 6 Rue Gît-le-Coeur, 75006 Paris, +33 (0)1 43 54 49 98, www.salledarmescoudurier.org | **Getting there** Metro to Saint-Michel (Line 4) or Odéon (Lines 4 and 10) | **Hours** By reservation, every day except Sun, 5pm–9pm. | **Tip** Don't miss Le Procope, 13 Rue de l'Ancienne-Comédie, the oldest café in Paris, founded in 1686 by the Italian Francesco Procopio Dei Coltelli.

33__The Curiosity Cabinet
For the nature-curious

It is one of the quirkiest collections in Paris, and you can check it out in the media library of the Museum national d'Histoire naturelle. The extremely wealthy Joseph Bonnier de la Mosson (1702–1744) was the heir of the private mansion of the Comte du Lude, situated at 244 Boulevard Saint-Germain. He had a passion for the sciences, which he never stopped feeding.

Over the course of his travels he brought back the most beautiful and original specimens that he was able to acquire. To expose the fruits of his research, he had the rooms of the second floor of his home transformed into a succession of curiosity cabinets: one dedicated to chemistry, others to anatomy, to medicine, to mechanics, to physics, and so on. In the two cabinets of natural history, he exhibited many animals – either in vials or taxidermied.

To build this remarkable collection, Bonnier de la Mosson called upon some of the best experts and engineers in France and Europe, and in 1739, he deemed it complete. But he didn't get to enjoy it very long. His tendency towards profligacy made not only his collection but ultimately his misfortune. In 1744, the gentleman died in total destitution at the age of 42.

His creditors tried to recoup their debts by auctioning off his precious cabinets. All the collections were dispersed except for the second cabinet of natural history, which included insects and other preserved animals – totaling five armoires acquired by the Comte de Buffon for the King's Cabinet.

After changing hands several times, the magnificent ensemble of wood carvings of Holland oak, classified as historical artifacts in 1979, are now part of the Museum national d'Histoire naturelle's media library, where the specimens are presented in their original state. In the stylized displays, you will find butterflies and beetles, shells and fossils, shark teeth and crocodile eggs.

Address Médiathèque du Museum national d'Histoire naturelle, 38 Rue Geoffrey-Saint-Hilaire, 75005 Paris, +33 (0)1 40 79 36 36 | **Getting there** Metro to Place Monge (Line 7) | **Hours** Mon & Wed–Fri 11am–7pm; Sat 9am–6pm. Free entry. | **Tip** If you like Irish pubs, head to Connolly's Corner after your visit (12 Rue de Mirbel, open every day noon–2am), the oldest pub on the Rive Gauche, known for its variety of brown ales and the neckties lining its walls and hanging from its ceilings. Clients are invited to take their own off upon entry, to symbolically abandon the stress and worries of the office.

34__The Dejean Market

Africa goes to the market

If you love cooking with exotic products, with flavors that evoke far-off places, head over to this market in the northeast of Paris, which has the advantage of being open every day except Monday. Here you will find the African community of the capital in all its diversity – they come to find the indispensable products of their homelands. Located right outside the exit of the Château Rouge Metro station, the Marché Dejean is really like a condensed version of Africa. In the 1980s, the neighborhood saw arrivals from Senegal, the Ivory Coast, Togo, Cameroon, Congo – all the western countries of the continent.

The stalls are mouth-watering. It is a ballet of colorful fruits – plantains, little-known vegetables like African cucumbers or horned melons, sweet potatoes, okra, cassava. The fish displays are also a main attraction, and take up a large portion of the stalls. The fish arrives fresh from Africa by plane, coming especially from the Casamance region in the south of Senegal, and from countries that border the Gulf of Guinea. You will see huge Nile perch, tilapia, *plapla*, horse mackerel, *thiof* (what grouper is called in Senegal), Sompat grunt, *thiekeme*. Here sea bream is called *zungaro*, *pagrus*, or "big eyes" (*gros yeux*). Fresh fish so foreign, some of them do not even have names in English!

The vendors sell their merchandise amidst total chaos. They bargain, they shout at each other, they greet each other. Some clients come specifically from the *banlieue* suburbs to restock their pantries with the food that remind them of their homelands.

But the Marché Dejean is not only for food. There are also hairdressers, who offer a million different ways of straightening and dying hair – some of which might not be the best for your health! And there are tailors there, too, along with popular clothing and cosmetic vendors.

Address Between 21 Rue des Poissonniers and 26 Rue Poulet, 75018 Paris | Getting there Metro to Château Rouge (Line 4) | Hours Open every day except Monday | Tip To maintain that glorious feeling of having traveled to another country, go down the Boulevard Barbès to the over-ground Metro station, Boulevard de la Chappelle. There you will find the least expensive market in Paris, which explains the crowds. Don't be shy – elbow your way through to find a good deal.

35 __ Delaville Café

An atmosphere of "tolerance"

Who would have thought it? Behind this prototypical Parisian bar-brasserie façade and its acid-colored logo, there used to be one of the naughtiest spots in Paris under the Second Empire. Formerly know as Le Marguery, this banquet-style restaurant was all the rage until the 1900s. But the draw wasn't only the food: come nightfall the place would transform itself into a "house of tolerance" – a very nice French way of saying it was a brothel. Back in the day, it was the go-to place for any man of a certain social rank worthy of the euphemism of "tolerance." The reputation of some of these brothels of the period – Le Sphinx or Le Chabanais, for example – came to be well-known beyond the borders of France: Edward VII, the future king of England, was himself partial to Le Chabanais.

If you are curious as to whether these joints have held onto the traces of their naughty pasts, go see for yourself at the Delaville Café at lunchtime or for Sunday brunch. The food is good, and even if the "tolerant" atmosphere has, for the most part, disappeared, there are traces of it that still remain. The mirrors, the ceiling mosaic, the central staircase with its marble columns – every classic brothel motif you can think of is still there at the Delaville.

The 1946 law that closed all brothels naturally demanded a profound transformation of these establishments in order to conceal their original function, which is why they are so hard to recognize these days for what they used to be. Most of this aspect of Paris' social history has disappeared, which makes the discovery of the Delaville Café all the more exciting. Without reflecting on those telltale decorative signs, there is nothing to signal that the place used to be a brothel. No doubt most Parisians that eat here do not even know about its history – ask the people at the table next to your's when you go!

Address 34 Boulevard de Bonne-Nouvelle, 75010 Paris, +33 (0)1 48 24 48 09, www.delavillecafe.com | **Getting there** Metro to Bonne Nouvelle (Lines 8 and 9) | **Hours** Every day 8:30am–2am | **Tip** The place pays tribute to its naughty past every Tuesday. In its private salons, a cabaret workshop is offered (to women only): cabaret dance classes, makeup and styling sessions, and striptease. Do you dare? Check online for details.

36__ The Doubméa-Paris Factory

Paris has its prince

"Jambon de Paris" must be from Paris, right? Actually, the name merely refers to a recipe delivered to us from the Gauls: it is salted white ham, boiled in water, boned, dressed, pickled, cooked for several hours in an aromatic vegetable stock, and served in the form of a block of 10 to 12 pounds. A sign of opulence for country folk during the Middle Ages, the ham quickly became a staple in the diet of city-dwellers. Around the time of World War I, the price of ham made in or around Paris doubled because of a new tax. As such, the "Jambon de Paris" designation stopped meaning much, as it began to be used by industrial cured meats. Nowadays, it usually takes the form of vacuum-packed meats sold in a supermarket.

But good news for Parisians: our favorite sandwich stuffer and *croques-monsieur* filling is once more starting to be made in Paris proper – and made very well. Doumbéa, at the top of Rue de Charonne, is the newest salted-meat-maker in the capital, preparing artisanal-style cured meats using local pork from Mayenne, Sarthe, and Bretagne. "Authentic, nothing but quality," says the boss Yves le Guel, who even won the quality seal from Saveurs Paris, Île-de-France. The secrets of his recipe are as follows: salt from Guérande, spices, a stock made from real fresh vegetables, no dyes or preservatives, and fewer polyphosphates that make ham retain water. The hand-injected brine is diffused throughout the meat, making it melt on your tongue with a delicate taste. The factory's bestselling product is *le Prince de Paris*: branded with an Eiffel tower and sliced in long generous slivers, it is sold in fine grocery shops and at a few caterers around town. Florian Le Guel, Yves' son who's being groomed to take over the place, is convinced: there's no match for his family ham. He serves it to friends for holiday meals.

Address 166 Rue de Charonne, 75011 Paris, +33 (0)1 43 70 58 05, www.jambondeparis.com |
Getting there Metro to Alexandre Dumas (Line 2) | Tip Le palais de la Femme, run by the Armée
du salut, is a home for women built in 1910 by the benefactor Amicie Lebaudy. It is a registered
landmark and can be visited on national holidays (94 Rue de Charonne, www.armeedusalut.fr).

37___L'Élysée Montmartre

The show must go on

The mythical Élysée Montmartre was twice destroyed by a fire – first in 1900, then in 2011. Its most striking element – a metallic roof structure designed by Gustave Eiffel and originating from the French pavillion of the 1889 World Fair – was destroyed in the first fire. But since its 2016 renovation, the theater has been topped with a new and even more elaborate metallic roof, which can be appreciated from the inside of the theater as well. On the building's façade you will notice a beautiful molding of a dancer – this came from the Mabille ballroom, another well-known theater of the 19th century located on what is now Avenue Montaigne.

Opened in 1807, the Élysée Montmartre became a cabaret around 1880 – that is to say a restaurant, concert hall, and theater wrapped into one. It was a popular joint that hosted *bals-guingettes*, or outdoor dances, where the rich danced alongside the poor. The neighborhood bohemians came for the cancan shows made famous by the dancer known as "La Goulue" – those high kicks and splits were hard to resist. The only male dancer in the troupe was named Valentin le Désossé, who was thin as a rake and worked by day as a notary. Toulouse-Lautrec came regularly to sketch this peripheral world that snubbed bourgeois morality. In 1870, the "Club de la Révolution" regularly held its sessions at the Élysée Montmartre. Later on it became a factory for postal balloons – which, no joke, were hot air balloons that delivered mail!

Nearly a century later, in 1968, Jean-Louis Barrault produced the play *Rabelais* here. In 1971, it was home to Philippe Khorsand's hit *Oh Calcutta!*, which was sold out for four years running. And shortly after, Coluche mounted *Le temps des cérises*, in which he played the violin while wearing boxing gloves. In 1997, Daft Punk had their first concert here. And so the eclectic reputation of the place lives on.

Address 72 Boulevard de Rochechouart, 75018 Paris, www.elysee-montmartre.com | Getting there Metro to Anvers (Line 2) | Tip Check out the façade at 86 Boulevard Rochechouart. The year of 1860 is inscribed on this beautiful building to mark the annexation of the village of Montmartre into the city of Paris.

38_Émil'Or

A secret atelier

In the heart of the 3rd arrondissement, hidden behind hip boutiques on a street known for being super *bobo* (bohemian-bourgeois), Monsieur Émile of Émil'Or will open his doors and let you discover one of the last remaining jewelry ateliers in the Marais.

In the 18th century, the departure of the nobility for chicer neighborhoods in the west of Paris vacated a number of mansions in the area. These were quickly inhabited by jewelers, who set up their ateliers in the interior courtyards. Their activity was prolific until the early 20th century: in 1930, Paris rounded up 75% of gold jewelers, and 96% of jewelers overall. After the war, the profession was industrialized and left the heart of most major cities. But the Marais held onto a number of jewelers like Monsieur Émile, who were determined to continue practicing their art.

Born of a family of jewelers from Fez, Morocco, Monsieur Émile arrived at age 17 in Paris, where he learned his trade next to the great goldsmiths of the time before opening his own shop. He has been here for 28 years now, on the same street, and he is happy to tell you his story. He will even reveal the secrets of his atelier and collaborate with you to make the jewelry of your dreams. Let your imagination run wild – Monsieur Émile can make anything from simple drawings!

If you would rather leave the designing to him, he can also suggest models from his catalogue, in various cuts of diamonds and precious stones. He will explain in detail all the steps of fabrication, from the making of the model to the setting. And if you have old jewels in gold or silver, bring them in. Monsieur Émile will inspect and weigh them carefully right in front of you, and then put them into a founder to salvage the metal. All of his original works are engraved with a stamp. Ready-made jewelry at very reasonable prices – yes, it still exists in Paris.

Address By appointment only – Monsieur Émile will give you his address once you get in touch, +33 (0)1 48 87 55 80, emilor@outlook.fr | **Tip** After your visit, walk around the neighborhood and check out the Galerie Perrotin, 76 Rue de Turenne, situated in an old mansion that has been magnificently restored.

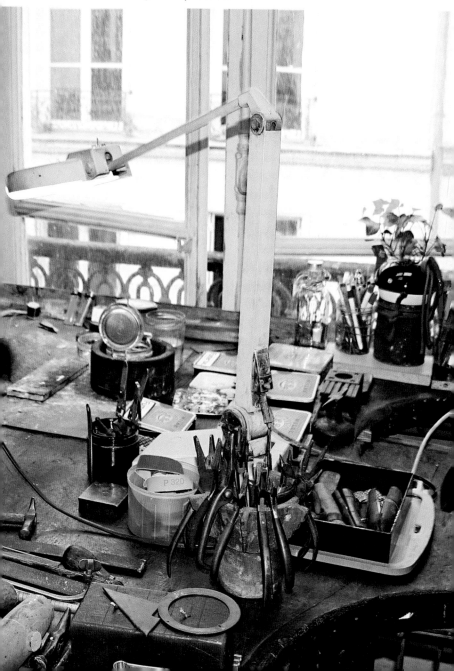

39 _Ennery Museum
Chimeras from the Far East

Behind the walls of this Avenue Foch mansion, you will find treasures from the Far East just waiting to be discovered. A visit to the place will feel like a trip back in time – almost nothing has been moved since the end of the 19th century.

Such were the wishes of the owner, Clémence d'Ennery, who built the home in 1875 for herself and her husband Adolphe, a successful playwright. She had to add on several wings in order to house her strange collection of objects from the Far East. "Strange" because Mme d'Ennery distinguished herself from other French collectors of Asian art of the time by "son goût du bizarre" (her taste for the strange), in the words of the Goncourt brothers.

But then again, chimeras, those mythical beasts made from parts of various animals, are themselves somewhat strange. And the particular combinations of Chinese and Japanese chimeras – half-lion, half-tiger, for example – appealed to Mme d'Ennery. Though she herself never explained her fondness for these fantastical creatures, her collection speaks for itself: there are more than 1,300 in the windows of the museum alone! Just under their watchful gaze you will also find her *netsuke*: tiny, intricately carved boxes worn on the belts of Japanese men to store small quantities of tobacco, money, or medicine, as their robes had no pockets. At the end of the 19th century, there weren't many collectors interested in *netsuke,* though these miniature sculptures are now very much in demand. Be sure to inspect them closely – some of them are pretty witty.

The childless Mme d'Ennery hoped to donate her collection to the state, but once she realized that her dream of having a room in her name at the Louvre was not going to happen, she transformed her home into a museum and left it to Georges Clemenceau, also an aficionado of Asian art, who made sure her house remained intact, as she had conceived it.

Address 59 Avenue Foch, 75010 Paris, +33 (0)1 56 52 53 44, www.guimet.fr/fr/
museedennery/histoire-du-musee-dennery | Getting there Metro to Porte Dauphine
(Line 2) or RER to Avenue Foch (Line C) | Hours Free guided tours Sat at 11:30am,
reservations by telephone or at resa@guimet.fr required | Tip The museum opened its
doors in 1908 and from then on was part of the Musée Guimet (Musée national des
arts asiatiques, 6 Place d'Iéna, 75116 Paris). A beautiful spot to discover if you're on
an Asian-art kick.

40___The Ermitage House
A Parisian folie in the Regency style

From the 17th century on, any Parisian aristocrat worth their salt had a *folie*, or country house, not far from the city. Just near the Porte de Bagnolet, in the Rue de Bagnolet's peaceful flower gardens, and at the corner of the Rue des Balkans, a beautiful old *folie* remains – the only vestige of the Bagnolet estate.

In the 18th century, the area was in the countryside. In 1719, Françoise-Marie de Bourbon, daughter of Louis XIV and wife of the Duke of Orléans (called the Régent), bought the Maison de Bagnolet. She added two wings onto the exterior façade and extended the park considerably, making it one of the most beautiful in the region. In 1738, it reached 80 hectares, most of which occupied Charonne land. The Duchess of Orléans had three *folies* built near the Maison by an architect named Serin. The Hermitage – now spelled "Ermitage" – was one of them.

The Ermitage was actually never meant to be occupied. As its big bay windows and the orientation of its rooms suggest, it was an indoor space made specifically to enjoy the nature surrounding it. The façade facing the garden still has three original arched windows. In the vestibule and the former gallery, the original wall murals remain, depicting the hermit saints for whom the pavilion is named.

In 1769, the chateau and two of the three *folies* were destroyed. Only the Ermitage remained. Bought in 1787 by the Baron de Batz-Lomagne, it served as a refuge to royalists who tried to help Louis XVI escape on the day of his execution, January 21, 1793. The 54 "conspirators of Charonne" were subsequently arrested and guillotined in the Place du Trône (now the Place de la Nation).

After belonging to the Assistance Publique hospital, since 1972 the home has been maintained by the Centre d'Action Sociale de la Ville de Paris, which aims to showcase the Ermitage's unique and endearing heritage.

Address 148 Rue de Bagnolet, 75020 Paris, +33 (0)1 40 24 15 95,
www.pavillondelermitage.com | **Getting there** Metro to Ourcq (Line 5) or Crimée
(Line 7) | **Hours** Thu–Sun (2nd week of Mar–mid-Dec, except Aug) 2pm–5:30pm;
guided evening visits with *apéritif de la duchesse* | **Tip** On the charming pedestrian street
called Rue Saint-Blaise, the bistro-wine-bar Le Casque d'Or pays homage to Simone
Signoret in the Jacques Becker film. It has a friendly atmosphere, where regulars come
with friends (15 Rue Saint-Blaise, 75020 Paris, +33 (0)1 43 71 31 64).

41__Evi Evane

The best taramasalata in Paris

I love Greece. The gods and the heroes of mythology have captured my imagination since I was a kid. Later on, I couldn't stop visiting the place, wandering all over the country by bus, by car, and even by foot. It is particularly nice off-season. I owe to a Greek friend of mine my discovery of Evi Evane, home to the best taramasalata in Paris!

Without colorants or cream, so smooth you can taste the cod eggs at the first bite, it has to be the best appetizer in the world! I often stock up on it, because apart from the restaurant on Rue Guisarde, Evi Evane owns two other places: a little caterer on Rue Saint-Placide and Evi Evane Mézès, which has been open on Rue Mazarine since 2015.

The place was started a dozen or so years ago by two sisters, Maria and Dina Nikolaou. They both hail from Kyrtoni, north of Athens, where they grew up eating traditional dishes cooked by their mother. They came to France to study in Paris and never left. While Dina is in the kitchen, Maria takes care of the floor. They have a kitchen in Kremlin-Bicêtre where they concoct their delish spreads, or *tartinables*: the divine taramasalata, eggplant pâté, olive pâté, and so on. Dina also appears on cooking shows in Greece, publishes cookbooks, and teaches gastronomy, while Maria runs the three Evi Evane joints. One of the most requested dishes is the moussaka, made with grilled eggplants to make it a bit healthier. As for the meat, it is minced right in the kitchen. One of the best desserts is the orange cake, prepared with real pressed oranges. Try it – it is irresistible! You can also shop some of their excellent products: honey from thyme plants in Crete, olives from Kalamata, organic saffron teas, Hellenic wines from some of the most renowned vineyards… It is all quality stuff, which makes sense – after all, Evi Evane means "to your health" in Ancient Greek!

Address Evi Evane Bistrot, 10 Rue Guisarde; Evi Evane Mézès, 66 Rue Mazarine; Evi Evane Traiteur, 20 Rue Saint-Placide, 75006 Paris, www.evievane.com | **Getting there** Metro to Mabillon (Line 10) | **Hours** Mon–Sat 11am–11pm | **Tip** A few steps from the station in Montparnasse, there's a bookstore that has been around since 1983. Its name means "connection" in Greek, and its owners Yannis and Françoise Mavroeidakos are dedicated to providing the link between Greek literature and Paris. (Librairie Desmos, 14 Rue Vandamme, 75014 Paris, +33 (0)1 43 20 84 04, Tue–Sat noon–7pm)

42 Ferrandi Paris

Not your ordinary student restaurant

My niece was a student at Ferrandi, one of the best culinary schools in Paris. They offer training in everything from cooking to baking to restaurant service. But it is not just a place of learning – you can taste the creations of the students and their professors in the restaurants run by the school. Just go to their website – that is the only way to make reservations. Simple enough, but one heads-up: you will probably have to reserve months ahead of time. At Ferrandi Paris (there's another campus in Jouy-en-Josas, in the Yvelines) – there are two dining options: *le Premier* and *le 28*. Once you set a date, all you have to do is show up on time: 12:30pm for lunch and 7:30pm for dinner. For 25€, 35€, or 45€, you can select a fixed menu that is guaranteed to put your taste buds to good use.

On the dining floor, the restaurant service students take care of you under the watchful eyes of their professors. They are training in the high art of French table-waiting: how to take orders, present impeccable dishes, and manage stress. And in the kitchen, there is not a dull moment. My niece tells me that every Thursday night, her class was made to prepare the restaurant meals under the supervision of students in their final year. They made everything from a chocolate piano to a tiramisu in the shape of a train to jellied oysters. The night of the jellied oysters, everyone got home and went to bed so late that they all slept through patisserie class the next morning. But since that was my niece's favorite, she was the only one who showed up awake and ready to work, and she managed to undertake all the tart-making for her entire class without getting caught.

Sometimes, her professor would bring students to do teatimes in major patisserie or luxury hotels. Other times, for lunch, they would all go eat at Mamie gateaux at 66 Rue du Cherche Midi, right near Ferrandi.

Address 28 Rue de l'Abbé-Gérgoire, 75006 Paris, +33 (0)1 49 54 28 00, www.ferrand-paris.fr | **Getting there** Metro to Saint-Placide (Line 4) | **Hours** *Le Premier*: lunch Tue–Fri, call for dinner inquiries; *le 28*: lunch Tue, Wed, and Thu. | **Tip** There are other culinary school restaurants in Paris, like Vatel: a great place to get a fancy meal at a meager price. Don't neglect the dessert menu! (122 Rue Nollet, 75017 Paris, +33 (0) 1 42 26 26 60)

43 __ The Fountain of the Fellah

A souvenir from Napoleonic Egypt

Paris is home to 262 fountains. The Fountain of the Fellah, in the neo-Egyptian style, is a souvenir from the Napoleonic Empire. Built in 1806 under the Decree of Saint-Cloud, an imperial decree ordering the creation of 15 fountains to improve the water supply of the capital, it managed to escape being destroyed by Haussmann's transformations of the city, and remained at its original location. The water that arrived here came from the Seine and was pumped by the Gros Caillou steam-pump, built in 1788 on the Quai d'Orsay by the Compagnie des Eaux des Frères Périer. But because of leaks in the neighboring subway station, Vaneau, the fountain has not run since 2005.

Known as the "Egyptian fountain," it was classified as an historical monument in 1972. The entire fountain recalls the door of an Egyptian temple, in front of which stands a man called "the fellah," meaning an Egyptian peasant. In spite of his modest condition, the man wears a Pharaoh's headdress, the nemes, and is clothed in a short pleated loincloth. Above him, in the niche, an imperial eagle with outstretched wings takes the place of the Behedeya, the winged solar disk of ancient Egypt.

The sculpture is inspired by the statue *Antinous as Osiris*, representing the 2nd-century Greek emperor Hadrian's "favorite" (lover). It was discovered in 1738 in Hadrian's Villa Adriana in Tivoli, near Rome. Osiris was the god of fertility and the plant kingdom. He was said to have been found dead, drowned in the Nile – and this was the same fate that befell Antinous when he was only 20 years old. Napoleon brought back the statue from his Italian campaign, and it was exhibited at the Louvre. With the fall of Napoleon's Empire, the statue was returned to Italy and put in the Vatican Museum. The statue you see today at the fountain was badly damaged and replaced by a copy in 1830.

Address 42 Rue de Sèvres, 75007 Paris | Getting there Metro to Vaneau (Line 10) | Tip Not far from the fountain, check out the entrance of the Vaneau station, constructed in 1923 in the art deco style, with its green and blue enameled tiles and two bright wrought-iron signs.

44_Foujita at the Japan House

Hidden treasures

The Cité Internationale Universitaire de Paris, a formidable pacifist creation of the 1920s that brings together 40 student residences and welcomes students of no fewer than 140 different nationalities, is well known. But have you ever had the chance to go inside any of the houses? These private residences are almost impossible to visit and their hidden treasures remain for the most part the exclusive benefit of those who live there.

The Japan House is an exception to this rule, and as long as you drop by during the building manager's hours with €2, he will open the doors and pull back the protective curtains from the wall at the end of the Great Hall, revealing two murals by Foujita, completed soon after the opening of the residence in 1929. These works are not well known, but they are sure to impress, whether you are a casual amateur of modern art or an enlightened admirer of the famous Japanese artist.

Foujita, who arrived in Paris in 1913, is one of the emblematic figures of the Parisian avant-garde of Montparnasse. A graduate of the School of Fine Arts in Tokyo, where he specialized in Western art, he quickly found great success among Parisian collectors. But once his fortune was made, the tax authorities got involved. It was an artist in the grips of great financial distress who accepted the commission from Satsuma, patron of the Japan House, though he left France afterwards in hopes of replicating his same success in his homeland.

The two murals, *The Horses* and *The Arrival of the Occidentals in Japan*, are a reflection of this period of his work, where he combines strong Western influences with traditional Japanese references in the hope of pleasing his fellow countrymen. Sure enough, success awaited him in Japan, where he became the most Western of the Japanese artists while remaining for us the most exotic of Parisian painters!

Address 7 C Boulevard Jourdan, 750014 Paris, +33 (0)1 44 16 12 12, www.ciup.fr/maison-du-japon | **Getting there** Tramway (Line T3a) or RER (Line B) to Cité Universitaire | **Hours** Mon – Fri 8:30am – 1pm and 2pm – 4:30pm | **Tip** Several minutes walk from the Cité Universitaire is Square de Montsouris, a small street perpendicular to the west side of the eponymous park, which is one of the most bucolic in Paris. Foujita owned a house there at number 3.

45_Galerie Vuitton

The treasure chests

To gain entry into the legendary atelier of the most famous luggage maker in the work, Louis Vuitton, you must show your credentials and check your bag at the door. From the entry hall, you can see the workshops where the luggage and all of the special orders are made. 177 craftsmen work here, most of them multi-skilled. Each worker is in charge of a product from scratch to finish.

The family venture started in 1859 when Louis Vuitton built this workshop in Asnières, five years after having opened his first shop in Paris. Very quickly, he made a name for himself creating pieces that boasted creative genius alongside good old-fashioned common sense. In 1860, for example, he replaced the curved top of trunks with a flat one, making it easier to pile them up. Later he replaced the leather usually used on trunks, which would be soaked through after a long outdoor journey on coaches, with a waterproof cloth.

So what did he do when his eponymous trunks, thanks to their huge success, became subject to mass counterfeit production? Well, Louis then came up with the grey Trianon canvas, followed by the striped canvas, and finally the checkered canvas. It was his son, Georges, who in 1896 invented the famous monogram pattern. Do you know how to recognize an authentic Vuitton trunk? The real ones have a lock with a serial number. If you lose your key, only the Vuitton workshops will be able to replace it.

The guided tour of the museum is itself a sort of treasure chest: all sorts of anecdotes are revealed, along with some beautiful original models. A particularly amusing throwback is the *faux-cul* or bustle-shaped bag: designed in 1996 by Vivienne Westwood as a tribute to the bustles worn by the most stylish ladies of 1860–1880. Finally, the visit leads you to the family house, remodeled in 1900 in the art nouveau style, which is just as stylishly elegant as you would expect.

Address 16 Rue Louis-Vuitton, 92600 Asnières-sur-Seine, +33 (0)9 77 40 40 77 | **Getting there** Metro to Gabriel Péri (Line 13) | **Hours** Reservation required, information online | **Tip** Once you are back in the real world, why not taste a bit of traditional French cuisine with farm-fresh products at La Petite Auberge (118 Rue de Colombes, in Asnières, every day except Monday).

46__Les Grands Moulins de Pantin

Untouched industrial heritage

You must come to admire these mills by night, when their tall silhouettes, dressed in violet and pink, are reflected off the waters of the Ourcq canal! At the end of the 19th century, the first mill was already here, equipped with 24 millstones that Abel Stanislas Leblanc, a miller from the Brie region, had had built. He had already anticipated how the location – right between the canal and the railroad – would be ideal.

In the 1920s, the Grands Moulins de Pantin company ordered the construction of enormous flour mills. They commissioned two architects from Strasbourg – Haug and Zublin – who designed eight-story silos built in the Alsatian style. A boiler room flanked by a coal silo, a railway platform, and a bakery completed the structure. At the peak of their activity, the Grands Moulins de Pantin produced 190,000 tons of flour per year.

Then came World War II and its bombings. On August 19, 1944, fire from the German anti-aircraft forces severely damaged the buildings. Repaired between 1945 and 1950, they resumed production little by little until the 1970s, when the consumption of bread in France began to decline. Around then, the Grands Moulins de Pantin adopted automated industrial production, but they eventually closed their doors in 2001. The buildings were bought by Menieur Immobilier, a subsidiary of Paribas, which decided to turn them in offices. The architects Bernard Reichen and Philippe Robert carried out the important work of restructuring the buildings in order to preserve the memory of the place. The three towers and the large broken roofs have all been preserved. The firebrick factory has been transformed into a cafeteria and the old engine room can still be seen in the middle of the glass-framed building. Even though two silos have been demolished, the third one overlooking the canal has been restored.

Address Rue du Débarcadère, 93500 Pantin | Getting there Metro to Ella Fitzgerald (Line 3b) or RER to Pantin (Line E) | Tip At the end of the canal near the Grands Moulins, there's a tall chimney that once belonged to the Leducq Laundry, which opened in that location at the end of the 19th century. Its business was helped along by the laundry detergent and soap makers, as well as the Eau de Javel disinfectant producers in Pantin. In 1967 it was bought by the Elis laundry company and is still functioning today.

47 La Grisette de 1830

Glory to the working girl

At the outlet of Canal Saint-Martin, the statue of a young girl sparks curiosity. Who is this girl, this "Grisette of 1830," with her modest half-smile and her miraculously voluminous bun sitting on top of her head? Not the most fashionable statue you've ever seen. But there is a reason for that: she takes us back to the world of Mimi Pinson, a character invented by Musset in 1845. In his book, the poor little worker-girl Mimi lives in an attic room that is too hot in the summer and too cold in the winter. She's a laundry-girl, a dressmaker, a fabric-dyer, a produce-seller – in short, she's a hard-working lass without any money: "Mimi Pinson is blonde as hell / And she's a blonde we all know well. / But she's only got one dress, / that poor little laundress! / And only one bonnet has she, / Fewer than the Emperor of Turkey. / But God wanted it that way / To make her good, that is what they say. / She couldn't even rightly pawn / That ugly dress that she has on."

In *Scènes de la vie de bohème*, also published in 1845, Henry Murget portrays a working girl, Grisette. She gets her name from the color of the long grey gown that she wore. "Grisette" was a thin fabric made of a combination of silk, wool, and string or cotton, and it was used to make the clothes of lower-class women.

Sculpted by Jean Descomps in 1911, the statue on Square Jules-Ferry was well received by the press at its inauguration: "State ministers had probably better praise the little worker who labors for her living rather than singing the vague memories of all of these district politicians for whom we so abusively dedicate bronze or marble statues as soon as they die!" mused a reporter for *Le Petit Journal*. If Grisette were to come back today she would no longer recognize the neighborhood where she sold her roses to passersby. There are no working folks along the canal – today it is mostly hipsters.

Address Square Jules-Ferry, 75011 Paris | Getting there Metro to République (Lines 3, 5, 8, 9, and 11) | Tip In the center of Square Jules-Ferry, whose flowers were chosen in homage to Grisette, a large fenced-off circular space can be spotted in the middle of the flowerbeds. It is an underground air vent.

LA GRISETTE
DE 1830

48___Halle Pajol
A unique eco-neighborhood

In the heart of "Marx Do" (Marx Dormoy for the uninitiated), a neighborhood in the north of Paris that is undergoing a veritable renaissance, you will find the Halle Pajol, a model eco-neighborhood. Decommissioned in 1992, the former warehouse of the SNCF national railroad was built in 1920 on the edge of the railroads coming from Gare du Nord. It was at first a refuge for the homeless. Then, artist ateliers and other businesses occupied it. Finally, it was acquired by the Mairie de Paris, which wanted to build a model urban center.

It is a hallucinating place, and an architectural gem – mere adjectives cannot do it justice. It took ten years of project studies and consultations to make this urban utopia spring forth from the site. The project was imagined by Françoise-Hélène Jourda, a pioneer of eco-architecture, who died in 2015 at the age of 59.

They managed to save the metallic structure as a sort of skeleton enveloping all the buildings, which were covered in wood and the saw-tooth roofs, most of which were preserved. These roofs have now allowed for the installation of 38,000 square feet of photovoltaic solar panels.

The Halle Pajol houses the Václav Havel library, stores, restaurants, shared office spaces and the Yves Robert youth hostel. From the balcony of its cafeteria, there is an unobstructed view: beyond the gardens and ponds and the elegant metallic frameworks, you can see the trains passing. The youth hostel, which produces its own electricity and that of neighboring buildings, also plays the eco card, asking its residents to respect the rules of the simple life: switch off your lights, only run the water you need from the faucet, and respect noise levels. All in the name of cohabitation! On nice days, the esplanade and the terraces of the bistrot on the side of the street are buzzing with concerts, festivals, and big barbecues.

Address 20–26 Rue Pajol, 75018 Paris | Getting there Metro to Marx Dormoy (Line 12) | Tip Wander around the Marché de la Chapelle, known as the "marché de l'Olive," at 10 Rue de l'Olive. It is a charming little covered market in the former Halle Baltard, with vendors offering exotic products, and a bunch of little cafés surrounding it.

49___The Hennebique Building
A concrete system

On Rue Danton, at the corner of the Place Saint-André-des-Arts, there is a rare architectural pearl dating from 1898. On its ceramic pillar reads an enigmatic inscription: "Système Hennebique," framed by two young half-naked girls with wings.

At the end of the 19th century, François Hennebique, a self-taught architect-entrepreneur from Belgium, made a name for himself using reinforced concrete. Apart from being both cheap and fire-resistant, Hennebique said of the material: "You can ask anything of reinforced concrete, and it can imitate anything."

Well-versed in marketing, Hennebique registered trademarks for his techniques and established a network of agents and dealers – in France, in Europe, then across the whole world. Between 1892 and 1921, he completed more than 20,000 projects! Houses, water towers, over 1,000 bridges, walkways, footbridges, theaters, industrial buildings, pools, brasseries, water treatment plants, manure cellars.

The Hennebique system was a hit, and it was recognized as such at the 1900 World Fair. As a result, Hennebique went on to patent a system based on the "particular combination of metal and cement for the creation of high-resistance beams" – a superb example of which can be found at 1 Rue Danton. Made entirely of reinforced concrete, it was conceived by the master himself, following the architectural plans of Édouard Arnaud. It was there that Hennebique set up his firm. In the offices, a hundred or so engineers and draughtsmen undertook thousands of projects per year. The building also housed several luxurious apartments, including that of the architect himself. He kept taking on more and more audacious projects – the Risorgimento Bridge in Rome, for example, and the Royal Liver Building in Liverpool (at the time the highest skyscraper in Euopre). Hennebique also left behind a rich archive of detailed documents.

Address 1 Rue Danton, 75006 Paris | **Getting there** Metro to Saint-Michel (Line 4) | **Tip** Hennebique was single-minded in his ideas. From Saint-Michel, it is worth hopping on the RER B and heading to Bourg-la-Reine to check out another of his spectacular projects. This one is a family villa completed in 1901, which the architect had made to live and work with his children. Terraces, ceiling-to-floor windows, suspended gardens, a 130-foot-high gravity-operated reservoir, Hennebique put his imagination to good use! (1 Avenue du Lycée-Lakanal)

50__ Hôtel Chopin

A hotel in a passageway

Right in the middle of the Passage Jouffrey, just next to a side entrance of the Musée Grévin, sits the Hôtel Chopin. A well-shielded little spot in one of the busiest neighborhoods in the capital, it benefits from an exceptional location. On its shabby and outdated façade is a clock typical of those that you would find in old covered passageways. Built in 1846, the hotel dates from the origin of the Passage Jouffrey, which is in fact one of the oldest in Paris. Landmarked as an historical monument, it was called Hôtel des Familles until 1970. Its sign was repainted with its current name in 2010 for the filming of Florian Henckel von Donnersmarck's *The Tourist*, with Angeline Jolie and Johnny Depp.

Its name pays homage to the composer who crossed the passageway regularly to go to the piano store called Pleyel. It is there that he is said to have met his mistress George Sand. It is true that, behind its *pension de famille*, or boarding-house vibe, the hotel is as romantic as you could wish for. And perfect for couples in need of the utmost discretion, as it will be nearly impossible for you to get caught: the doors of the Passage Jouffrey are closed from 9:30 at night to 7:00 in the morning. No need for a "Do Not Disturb" sign on your door at the Hôtel Chopin – it is on lockdown every night.

A good tip: make a reservation and ask for a *mansarde* room on the top floor, which gives an extraordinary view out of the windowed walls of the roof. Far off to the left, you can spot the dome of the Musée Grévin Theater that adjoins the passageway. Fans of 19th-century architecture will appreciate the rib-shaped metallic structure and will learn that Passage Jouffrey was the first to be heated through its floors. In the middle of the alley, you will also notice the grates overlooking the Metro, which runs the whole length of the passage.

Address 46 Passage Jouffrey (entrances at 10–12 Boulevard Montmartre and 9 Rue de la Grange Bâtelière), 75009 Paris, +33 (0)1 47 70 58 10, www.hotelchopin.fr | **Getting there** Metro to Grands Boulevards (Lines 8 and 9) | **Hours** Open every day | **Tip** Nearby you will find the Passage Verdeau and there, the Drouot auction house – 16 galleries and daily auctions between 11am and 6pm. It is a favorite of art collectors.

51 Hôtel des Grandes Écoles

The countryside in a hotel

When I was a student, I lived in a former maid's quarters on the top floor of a building on the Place du Panthéon. The room was tiny, and I had to walk up the eight flights of the servant's staircase to get there. But I loved walking around the Montagne Sainte-Geneviève, and I am still just as fond as ever of this tiny corner of Paris that dates back to the Roman period.

Rue du Cardinal Lemoine is just steps away. At the end of a court lined with low stone walls, there's an adorable hotel whose windows look out onto the greenery as if you were really in the countryside. The Hôtel des Grandes Écoles is a vast mansion with pink stucco walls, surrounded by tall trees and a flowering garden. When the weather is nice, you can have breakfast *à la française* under the parasols in the cobblestone courtyard, which is spacious enough to not feel hemmed in, as you so often can in this overcrowded city.

The hotel's rooms, with their painted floral wallpapers and old furnishings, give off a retro 1960s vibe. It is like staying in your granny's guest bedroom. And to further provoke your feeling or temporal displacement, all televisions are banned from the place. The owner, who has been in charge for years, has formed a personal relationship with many of the clients. Once you have tried it out, it might just be hard to go stay anywhere else. And the prices are pretty low for a hotel of this caliber. It is best to make reservations, because it fills up regularly with tourists. And you couldn't ask for a better location – the neighborhood is filled with treasures. The Place de la Contrescarpe and Rue Mouffetard heading east, the Place Maubert and its bustling market going north and the Panthéon and its great men – and women! – of the vast esplanade. Not to mention the charming Rue de l'Estrapade behind the 5th arrondissement *Mairie*. It is a great spot to really get to know Paris.

Address 75 Rue du Cardinal-Lemoine, 75005 Paris, +33 (0)1 43 26 79 23, www.hotelgrandes-ecoles.fr | **Getting there** Metro to Cardinal Lemoine (Line 10) | **Hours** Open all year, prices and availability online | **Tip** You must take a tour of the Piano Vache (Mon–Sat 6pm–2am), a rock 'n' roll institution since 1969! You will bump into high-school students from Henri-IV, the most prestigious school in the Latin Quarter, students from the Sorbonne, and old May '68ers who've been loyal customers since way back when.

52__Hôtel Païva
The splendor of a courtesan

It is hard to describe the Païva mansion on the Champs-Elysées: Lavish? Luxurious? Ostentatious? Its owner, a famous courtesan, had an axe to grind with life – and boy, did she grind it!

Born into poverty in Moscow in 1819, the Polish Esther – later Thérèse – Lachmann was married at 17, but ran away soon after to Paris with a passing stranger. She started making acquaintances, and soon she was one of the most famous *demi-montaines* of the capital.

The pianist Henri Hertz fell madly in love with her, and she managed to get her hands on his large fortune. Poor Hertz had no noble title, but Thérèse solved this bother by marrying the Portuguese Marquis de Païva Araujo, whom she left the very next day. Scorned, mocked, and ruined financially, the marquis killed himself shortly afterwards.

In 1852, the marquise set her sights on a rich cousin of Chancelor Bismarck, the Count Guido Henckel von Donnersmarck, who offered her a yearly allowance of two million francs. But forget income: his real gift was building her a mansion on the brand-new Avenue des Champs-Élysées – the perfect metaphor for the astonishing rise of the once-destitute exile. A bounty of bronze, marble, ceramic, mosaic, woodwork, and gold, it is an extraordinary decorative example of the Second Empire, where a monumental staircase in golden onyx competes with a powder room decked out with a chimney-fountain.

Alexandre Dumas, *fils*, upon seeing the building in 1867, scoffed: "It is almost finished. Nothing left to do but to put in the sidewalk!" La Païva, as she was called from then on, welcomed the crème de la crème of literary society into her salon: the Goncourt brothers, Gautier, Sainte-Beuve. Her wild parties were enormously popular. But fate eventually caught up with her. Accused of spying after the war of 1870–1871, she retired to Silesa with the Count of Donnersmarck, her then-husband, where she died in 1884.

Address 25 Avenue des Champs-Élysées, 75008 Paris | Getting there Metro to Franklin D. Roosevelt (Lines 1 and 9) | Hours Property of the Travellers Club, €6 entry, reservation required at www.paris-capitale-historique.fr/visite/hotel-paiva | Tip At her marriage to the Portuguese count, La Païva received as a gift from her new husband yet another mansion, at 28 Place Saint-Georges – also a charming address. At the time of its construction in 1840, the house caused a scandal because its neo-Renaissance façade was so overcrowded with details: shells, medallions, griffons, cherubs, and other statuettes were united in a surprising ensemble.

53__Hôtel Saint-James Paris
The first airfield in Paris

I have known the charming director of this château-hotel for twenty years now. So whenever I feel like seeing the Hôtel Saint-James, with its private garden and hot-air balloons, I just pick up my phone and call her.

It is a beautiful mansion from the end of the 19th century constructed by the widow of Adolphe Thiers, the second president of France, who used it to house the Fondation Thiers in homage to her husband. The goal? To give scholarships to brilliant but penniless students to that they could devote themselves entirely to their studies without having to work. In 1985, the foundation moved to Place Saint-Georges, in the 9th arrondissement. For a few years, its first home was bought and sold by various British companies. For a while it became the Saint James Club, where Bernard Rapp recorded his hit show *L'Assiette anglaise*.

The Hôtel Saint-James began its next life in 2008, when its new owners called in the renowned decorator Bambi Sloan, who has lived between New York and Paris since her childhood. Known for remixing bohemian and surrealist finds, all of Sloan's projects bear the indelible mark of her wacky style. She loves using unexpected colors, staging off-the-wall scenes, and creating hilarious universes of style based on the most improbable pairings. The result is always jarring but brilliant.

For the hotel terrace, she came up with plant-covered furniture in painted metal, mini-greenhouses, and huge hot-air balloons – a reminder that at the same location where the house was built in the 19th century, there was also Paris' first airfield, where the balloons took off.

If you prefer being indoors, you should definitely settle into one of the club chairs at the bar. The setting is so deliciously English, and right near a library filled with gorgeous old books: sit down and try one of the house cocktails. You might just forget you aren't in London.

Address 43 Avenue Bugeaud, 75116 Paris, +33 (0)1 44 05 81 81, www.saint-james-paris.com | **Getting there** Metro to Porte Dauphine (Line 2) or RER to Avenue Foch (Line C) | **Hours** Bar and terrace open from 7pm; Sunday: brunch for non-members of the club, free entry for hotel guests. | **Tip** The entrance to the Porte Dauphine station is topped with a magnificent glass dragonfly by Hector Guimard (the old-fashioned type of Metro awning that resembles a splayed rice-paper fan). It is the only *aedicula* of this kind that remains in Paris.

54 Indochinese Buddhist Temple

A home for the gods

Most people know about Paris' little Chinatown in the 13th arrondissement, a neighborhood teeming with exotic shops. But there's a lot more to discover nearby, if you're willing to venture under the concrete ground of the Olympiades area.

To get there, you will start on the Avenue d'Ivry. Look for the red drinking fountain (the only Wallace drinking fountain in Paris that is painted red). Just beyond the fountain, you will spot the discreet entrance to Rue du Disque – that is the street you want.

At number 37, Buddha is waiting to welcome you into his temple. Opened in 1989 by the A.R.F.O.I (Association of Residents in France of Indochinese Origin), the temple was originally an underground parking lot that became vacant at the time the entry system was automatized. Sure, it is a far cry from traditional Buddhist temple architecture, but those neighborhood residents who come here to worship have learned how to adapt. After all, it is all a matter of ritual.

A consecration ceremony transformed the space into a home for the Divinities. And so now you will find here, along with Buddha, the statues of Avalokitevaśra (the incarnate of compassion), Maitreya (the Buddha of the future), and the emperor Zhenwu (the Taoist figure embodying the mix of Buddhist and Taoist beliefs in Southeast Asia).

If you are wondering why there are huge bags of rice on the floor near the statues, there's a noble explanation. According to Asian tradition, they are left there as offerings to the gods, but they are also distributed as free meals to the neediest of the community on holy days.

Don't miss the photos on the wall of the Chinese New Year festivities: the A.R.F.O.I. organized the first dragon parade in the neighborhood in 1989, which remains a popular tradition today. Ask the caretaker for the date of the next one.

Address 37 Rue du Disque, 75013 Paris, +33 (0)1 45 86 80 99, www.arfoi-paris.com | **Getting there** Metro to Olympiades (Line 14) | **Hours** Every day 9am–6pm | **Tip** A question haunting you about the future? Go ask the chopsticks! They can be found on certain altars: shake them until one of them pops up, look at the number on that one and go find the corresponding sheet of paper at the nearby table. Then all you have to do is read and interpret the message. (But for that, you will probably need a friend who speaks the language!)

55 La Java

A legendary ballroom

One Thursday night, a sudden urge to go dancing led my friend and I to the "Bal des Martine" at La Java, the legendary ballroom in the basement of the Palais du Commerce. The building is an art deco construction dating from 1924 that has been landmarked as an historical monument since 1994. The space itself is totally unique: a commercial gallery constructed over three levels, with walkways around a central patio. The interior is lit up by glass flooring and tiles. The escalator tower above the entrance to La Java, for its part, is illuminated by splendid stained glass. In 1925, it was home to about fifty stores and ateliers, not to mention the Parisian hairdresser's union and, most importantly, to La Java.

The room is named for a popular waltz that reigned in dancehalls all over Paris. Before World War II, it was also a popular place for the middle classes to go slumming (and sometimes pick up hookers). Closed in 1940 then reopened in 1943, La Java managed to restore its original spirit, where people danced the traditional waltz alongside the Java to popular tunes of the day. Fréhel and Édith Piaf made their debuts here, trading little songs for a warm plate of lentils and a few *sous*. The wine was cheap and the stage could be wheeled in and out according to the needs of the night. Django Reinhardt went to La Java – they say it was here that he first heard both jazz and accordion music, and that his "gypsy jazz" was the fruit of these encounters.

In 1968, La Java was taken over by Jacques Morino, an Argentine conductor and former tango music specialist. La Java adapted to the tastes of the times by programming rock'n'roll and underground groups.

In the 1990s, with the arrival of world music, the club became a mecca for salsa. Since 2006, a new team has turned it into a late-night hangout and ballroom, with shows and concerts for young clubbers.

Address 105 Rue du Faubourg-du-Temple, 75010 Paris, +33 (0)1 42 02 20 52 | Getting there Metro to Belleville (Lines 2 and 11) or Goncourt (Line 11) | Hours Available at www.la-java.fr | Tip Go up Rue de Belleville until you find number 72, in the 20th arrondissement, where a plaque reminds you that right on the steps of this house, Édith Piaf was born into total destitution.

56_Jérome Seydoux-Pathé Foundation

An atrium with a backstory

Who would think that behind the somewhat dull façade, is a 5-story atrium? In this once working-class neighborhood, a theater was built in 1869. Auguste Rodin, who was a student at the École des Beaux-Arts, was hired to sculpt the façade: on it you will see two characters, Tragedy (the man) and Comedy (the woman). Inside this Italianate theater with 800 seats, mainstream popular plays attracted huge crowds. In 1906, they started showing documentary films there. In 1934, the theater was replaced by the Gaumont-Gobelins-Rodin cinema, which remained until 2003 before being turned into a warehouse.

Serious uncertainties reigned over the fate of the place during these years. The Fondation Jérome Seydoux-Pathé came onto the scene around then, as the Pathé brothers' businesses historically took part in the invention of film before turning into the world's largest film equipment and production company. The Gaumont-Gobelins-Rodin establishment was razed to the ground except for the façade to make way for the Renzo Piano-designed atrium – a structure that no one feels indifferent about. You can see it from the outside if you are on the sidewalk across the street on Avenue des Gobelins. Sophie Seydoux, the wife of Jérôme, the co-president of Pathé, had asked the architect to "construct a magical lantern in the heart of Paris."

The luxurious interior, with its happy mix of wood and steel, houses the Charles Pathé projection room devoted to silent films, a gallery of 150 film cameras that trace back over a century of the "7th art," a center for research, and exhibition spaces for shows in homage to cinema. The richness of the collections conserved by the foundation is very impressive. All of it is open to the public, with or without a guided tour.

Address 73 Avenue des Gobelins, 75013 Paris, www.fondation-jeromeseydoux-pathe.com | Getting there Metro to Les Gobelins (Line 7) | Hours Tue–Fri 1pm–7pm; Sat 10am–7pm | Tip To all board game lovers: Oya Café is waiting for you! In this former grocery store, more than 500 board game from all over the world are at your disposal. And the owners never stop finding new ones. Come alone or with family, and wile away the hours (25 Rue de la Reine-Blanche, 75013 Paris, +33 (0)1 47 07 59).

57_Jim Morrison's Building
Tracking down an idol

You may have visited his grave in the Père-Lachaise cemetery – the fourth most-visited site by tourists in Paris – but have you ever been to see the apartment where Jim Morrison was found dead the morning of July 3, 1971?

Jim and his girlfriend Pamela Courson moved into the fourth floor (the right-hand apartment) of this average-looking building in May 1971. The singer had fled the United States, where he was being threatened with prison time for indecent exposure during a concert in Miami. He also came to Paris for inspiration, but at 27 years old, he was already unrecognizable and very sick from the hard drugs he had been using.

What really happened from July 2 to July 3? The facts are controversial. Officially, Pamela found Jim in the morning at 5am in the bathtub, dead from heart failure. But another story suggests that he was discovered around 2:30 in the morning in the bathroom of Rock'n'Roll Circus, a club in the Saint-Germain-des-Près, dead of an overdose after having mixed too much vodka with a very pure dose of heroin. Terrified of his joint being the site of a scandal, the owner of the bar supposedly asked the dealers to take the singer back home.

The sad fate of Jim Morrison marked the end of a dazzling career of one of the biggest rock bands of the 20th century. Active from 1965 to 1973, The Doors did not survive long after the death of their poet. Jim had recorded six albums between 1967 and 1971, the last being *L.A. Woman*. And in the few months he spent in Paris before his end, he also managed to leave his mark in his little neighborhood: at the restaurant at 18 Rue Beautreillis, at the wine store at number 25 of the same street, and even at the local cheese shop at 43 Rue Saint-Antoine. Apparently he also loved taking refuge in the Place des Vosges, at the Père-Lachaise cemetery, and in several of the neighborhood bars.

Address 17 Rue Beautreillis, 75004 Paris | **Getting there** Metro to Saint Paul (Line 1) or Sully-Morland (Line 7) | **Tip** Check out the courtyards of the Village Saint-Paul (entrances can be found at Rue Saint-Paul, Rue de l'Ave-Maria, Rue Charlemagne, and Rue Jardins Saint-Paul) with its galleries, antique shops and boutiques, and its bistros. Flea markets are set up several times a year (www.levillagesaintpaul.com).

58__Kata

A magical movie theater

The street-level space is lined with enormous bins filled with shoes for sale at unbeatable prices. But once you go into the building, you will discover an enchanting place straight out of another era. One level up from the heaps of footwear, there is a fabulous theater with a balcony, columns, gorgeous ornate woodwork, and golden mouldings. On the stage, behind the red velvet curtain, Kata's owner, who took over the place in 1988, has installed an interior fresco in homage to what goes on below: it is a painting of a bulldozer pushing mountains of shoes and piles of shoeboxes.

The place was formerly a movie theater called Barbès Palace, the kind of *cinéma du quartier* that just does not exist anymore today. Open from 1914 to 1985, it remains mostly intact. A wide, windowless façade can be found on the other side of the building at 9 Rue des Poissonniers, but the interior is far more baroque: it was designed in the style of an Italian theater, and it is able to hold up to 1,200 people. Above the pilasters, the initials "BP" (Barbès Palace) are still visible. In fact, the place hasn't changed at all in a century – what a miracle! But in spite of the efforts of a group of cinephiles known as Eldorado, the building hasn't yet been landmarked as a historical monument.

It is too bad, too, because besides the décor, the place has a rich history within this very commercial neighborhood. In 1920, a show would start with the news, followed by a short comic film, then two features and a serial episode – all interspersed with advertisements and an orchestra during intermission. In the 1960s, the Barbès showed blockbusters, adventure films, thrillers, epics, and detective movies. Thursday afternoons were for kids and Saturday afternoons for families. From the 1970s on, it offered double features pairing action films with erotica. And on July 30, 1985, its curtain closed for good.

Address 34 Boulevard Barbès, 75018 Paris | Getting there Metro to Château Rouge
(Line 4) or Barbès – Rochechouart (Lines 2 and 4) | Hours Mon–Sat 10am–7pm | Tip
At 179 Boulevard Magenta, the *Le Louxor* movie theater (see ch. 64) is another
emblematic theater that was open from 1921 to 1983 and that reopened in 2013.

59 __ The Lady Barber of Paris
Making men look better

Lady barber? No way – only men are barbers! Well, except for Sarah, the Lady Barber. And actually, the only female barber in Paris!

She decided on her future when she was eight years old, when she would watch her Kabyle grandfather shave himself in front of the mirror. While admiring the precision of his movements maneuvering the razorblade, her future revealed itself to young Sarah: "I'm going to be a barber," she said.

She started by getting her diploma in hairdressing for men and women, then trained with barber visionaries such as Jean-Louis Bourasseau and Osan Turak, who taught her this fundamental lesson: "If you can shave a thick Turkish beard, you can shave anybody!" She credits her two mentors with transforming her into what she is today – a veritable star in her profession. She is in such demand that men have to wait between a month and a half and two months to get an appointment with her!

Her craft is anything but simple. It takes at least a year to get used to styling men because there are so many techniques: fading, layering, handling the razorblade – a dangerous weapon in the hands of a novice.

In 2000, Sarah decided to fly with her own wings. She opened her first salon on Rue Condorcet, which was so successful that in 2014 she opened another. This second one resides in a venerable house from the 14th century near Les Halles. It is a great spot, with its arched doorways of cut stone. You can see all the men waiting behind a big window.

Across the two salons, Sarah now has 22 employees. And since 2012, at the Centre de Formation de Nanterre, she's been training other salon owners in the art of barbering, which has not been taught for 30 years.

Her goal, quite simply, is to make men look better. At the Barbière de Paris, they also offer steam shaving, beard makeup, beard extension, and torso sculpture (where you can, no joke, get a fake six-pack drawn on).

Address 7 Rue Bertin-Poirée, 75001 Paris, +33 (0)1 40 26 01 01; 14 Rue Condorcet, 75009 Paris, +33 (0)1 45 26 92 45, www.labarbieredeparis.com | **Getting there** Metro to Poissonnière (Line 7) | **Hours** Mon–Fri 9am–6pm | **Tip** Two steps from the Barbière, there is a time-honored brasserie opened by an Alsatian family at the end of the 19th century, and still going strong. Le Zimmer, magnificently redecorated by Jacques Garcia, has maintained its beautiful ceiling and its floral décor (1 Place du Châtelet, +33 (0)1 42 36 74 03, www.lezimmer.com).

60___Léon the Lamppost
A streetlight from the past

What I like most about being in a city is finding those secluded places where you feel like you could be in the countryside! The Sentier du Tir, located in a tranquil neighborhood just steps away from *périphérique*belt highway, is one of those. On a pedestrian-only path, bordered by several old houses, some of which have maintained beautiful gardens, there is a neat old historical monument named Léon the Lamppost.

Léon is the only survivor of the bygone era of gaslight streetlamps to be found in the Paris region. In fact, there are only two left in all of France. The second hails from Sarlat, in the Dordogne region in the Southwest of France. Léon's survival is due to his long being the object of careful attention and loving care. He was saved in the 1970s by an association of local residents, Les Amis de Léon, which used all their force to oppose his electrification. Their obstinacy paid off: Léon kept his Auer gas burner, which continues to burn 24 hours a day. In fact, his survival requires him to stay illuminated 24 hours a day to avoid the slow deterioration that comes from being lit and extinguished all the time.

From dusk on, Léon distinguishes himself from other streetlights in the passage thanks to his romantic orange halo – an aura straight out of the 19th century. His more contemporary streetlamp peers have to content themselves with the cold white light of modernity. Check out his little windows and you will spot the names of the inventors of various gas lighting systems: the Frenchman Philippe Lebon, the Brit William Murdoch, and the Austrian Carl Auer. There are also two dates marking its history: 1785, when Lebon made the first gas lighting with wood distillation, and 1880, the beginning of electricity – which could have signaled the death of this guardian of the past.

But lucky for Léon, his protectors have prevailed and so he's stuck around.

Address Sentier du Tir, 92240 Malakoff | Getting there Metro to Malakoff – Plateau de Vanves (Line 13) or to Didot (Line T3a) | Tip Go look at the *empêche-pipi* (or pee-preventer) at 14 Rue Ernest Renan. Perpendicular to Sentier du Tir, Rue Ernest Renan is home to this conical and convex brick structure, with a plaque on the corner of the wall declaring it's purpose: to create splashes back onto the pants of men who dare relieve themselves in the street.

61__Liberté Ménilmontant
The boulangerie that shows everything

Wandering around the Ménilmontant neighborhood one Sunday, my gaze suddenly falls onto a beautiful space where all the tables are filled with people feasting on an enormous brunch... Should I go in? On one side of the room there are two gigantic ovens. On the other, the pâtisserie display case looks pretty appetizing.

Then I recognize Benoît Castel – the chef of this convivial spot – who is chatting with customers. His career path is enviable: after training in Bretagne, where he is from, and in Paris, he worked for Hélène Darroze and the Hôtel Costes before becoming head pastry chef at La Grande Épicerie de Paris. From there he called a good portion of his team to join him in starting his own venture.

Open since 2014, Liberté Ménilmontant has allowed Castel to go back to his roots a bit, as first he cut his teeth in Paris at the Pâtisserie de l'Église on Rue du Jourdain.

Liberté Ménilmontant privileges proximity with its clients, which is why its magnificent oven is totally visible from the street. Standing outside, you can see bread baking and rotisserie chickens spinning for Sunday brunch. Built in 1974, the oven was formerly used by the famous baker Bernard Ganachaud, who in 1979 was dubbed the *Meilleur Ouvrier de France*, or "the best worker in France." He is also the guy who invented the *flûte Gana* baguette. Castel bought the shop straight from Ganachaud.

In the Liberté Ménilmontant pâtisserie, everything is made on premises right before your eyes. Castel regularly visits all of his various locations to check in with customers and make sure everything's running smoothly. And for Sunday brunch, organized as self-service, he prepares a buffet of breads and *viennoiseries*, along with savory tarts, and hot dishes that vary each week – rotisserie chicken, *blanquette de veau, boeuf bourguignon* – and lots of other things that I will let you discover yourself.

Address 150 Rue de Ménilmontant, 75020 Paris, +33 (0)1 46 36 13 82 | **Getting there** Metro to Jacques Bonsergent (Line 5) | **Hours** Wed–Fri 7:30am–8pm; Sat 8am–8pm; Sun 8am–6pm, Sunday brunch at 11am, 1pm, and 3pm | **Tip** In Paris, Benoît Castel has a few other establishments where the baking is also open to the viewing pleasure of passersby: Liberté Vinaigriers, 39 Rue des Vinaigriers, 10th arrondissement, +33 (0)1 42 05 51 76; Liberté Les Galeries Lafayette Gourmet, 35 Boulevard Haussman, 9th arrondissement, +33 (0)1 40 23 52.

62 __ Lisch Station

A lost station

If you still do not know about the Lisch station, you might want to hustle. Located at a terminus, just opposite the Bois-Colombes station – only the train tracks separate them – it has been falling apart for years in spite of the calls put out by those concerned with its fate. And yet, this old station is quite moving, with its magnificent glazed-ceramic panels and its perfectly balanced architecture. It belongs to SNCF Réseau (the national railway company) and is named after its architect, whose first name was Juste. From Juste Lisch to a just cause – now there's an idea for a restauration project.

Let's take a trip back to the World Fair (or Exposition Universelle) of 1878: at the corner of Avenue de Suffren and Quai d'Orsay, the Champ-de-Mars landing stage was there to welcome visitors. The brand-new station consisted of a metal substructure with a stone base. Black, yellow and red bricks and ceramic tiles with vivid colors brightened up its tall façade.

In 15 years and over the course of two World Fairs (1878 and 1889), six million passengers passed through the station. But in 1897, following a project to build a new stop on the Invalides Esplanade, it was dismantled and then reassembled piece by piece at its present location, on the grounds belonging to the Compagnie de l'Ouest, where it was used as a warehouse and an annex. But between 1924 and 1936, it was put back into service, becoming the last stop of the electricity-powered Paris-Bois-Colombes line. In 1937, with the creation of the present Bois-Colombes station, it slowly began to deteriorate.

It took a long relentless battle for the station to be registered in 1985 in the inventory of historical monuments. These days, an association known as "Opération Renaissance" has taken it upon itself to fight for the restauration of the Lisch station, which has been severely damaged over time.

Address Impasse des Carbonnets, 92600 Asnières-sur-Seine, www.garelisch.fr | Getting there RER to Bois-Colombes (Line J) | Tip Across from Impasse des Carbonnets, go into the bar-tabac and walk all the way to the back to find a full-length portrait of Louix XV! It reminds you that this café, once called Le Louix XV, was opened in 1856 when the Gare de Bois-Colombes first opened.

63_Little India

Amid saris and cardamom

If you walk along the Rue du Faubourg-Saint-Denis between the Gare du Nord and the La Chapelle Metro station, in the north of the 10th arrondissement and just bordering the 18th, you will not fail to notice the number of Indian shops. The better known, if more touristy, enclave is found in the Passage Brady in the southern part of the 10th. There you will feel like you have traveled to a far-off land, surrounded by colorful saris, henna boutiques, and the smell of curry, cardamom, and incense.

The first Indian shop in the area was a grocery store opened in 1976 by a certain Antoine Ponnoussamy, originally from Pondicherry. Since then, over a dozen Pakistani restaurants have set up shop in the Passage. The nearby Rue Jarry feels even more like being on a little street in Karachi. You should also check out the Hindu temple Sri Manicka Vinayakar Alayam at 17 Rue Pajol in the 18th arrondissement. It is dedicated to Ganesh, the god with the head of an elephant and the body of a child, who is one of the most popular in India. Three times a day, at 10am, noon, and 7pm, they do a *puja*, or worship ceremony, symbolizing the communion between the gods and the world. On Fridays and weekends there are the *abhishekam*, sacred baths offered to the divinities. The worshippers here will welcome you with generosity, asking you only one small favor – to take off your shoes at the entrance.

Entry into the spiritual realm will probably not prevent you afterwards from returning to the joys of material goods. For example, you might want to try out one of the little cafeterias in the area where you can eat a nice fresh meal prepared before your eyes. We especially like Ganesah Corner, located at 16 Rue Perdonner. But look out – it is very spicy! And if you want try your hand at Indian cuisine at home, VT Cash & Carry is a convenience store where you will find all the products you will need.

Address Hindu Temple Sri Manicka Vinayakar Alayam, 17 Rue Pajol, 75018 Paris, www.templeganesh.fr; Passage Brady, entrance between 46 and 48 Rue du Faubourg-Saint-Denis, above the Gare du Nord, 75010 Paris; Rue Jarry, 75010 Paris | **Getting there** Metro (Lines 4, 5, and 7) or RER (Lines E and P) to Gare de l'Est | **Tip** If you are curious about Indian pastries, and specifically those from the south of the country, Ganesha Sweets (191 Rue du Faubourg Saint-Denis or 16 Rue Perdonnet) is one of the best places to go. They offer *jangri*, recognizable by their orange color, and *laddu*, little dumplings that are served for marriages as *prasadam*, or food eaten as a religious offering to Krishna.

64___Le Louxor

An Egyptian cinema

If the association Les Amis du Louxor had not fought relentlessly for years, there is no doubt that this mythical cinema would have been destroyed!

It is an absolutely gorgeous building, with its Egyptian frescoes, and even more so when night falls and it is all lit up. Inaugurated in 1921 in what was formerly a Haussmann building, it came into being right at the same time as film really started taking off. That was the era when Paris exploded with palatial movie-theaters, and sure enough, the Louxor can seat almost 1,200 spectators.

Named after the city built by Thebes in what is now southern Egypt, Le Louxor was constructed as a homage to that ancient culture at a time when Egyptomania was all the rage in Paris. They called in a talented decorator, Amédée Tiberti, to make the stencil paintings and the interior bas-reliefs. It is an art-deco take on Ancient Egypt, with floral motifs on the façade and lotus and papyrus pyramids done by the Gentil and Bourdet factory. The corner façade is the most beautiful, made up of blue, black, and gold mosaics, and decorated with winged beetles, cobras, and a winged sun. In the main room, the beams of the ceiling are covered in fantastical hieroglyphs, like something out of an Egyptian dream.

Since its opening, the programming has been varied and original: comical short films, serial films such as *Les Mystères de Paris*. In the 1970s and 1980s, Le Louxor primarily showed Indian and Arab films, especially Egyptian, in their original versions. In 1981, the façades of the roof were landmarked as historical monuments. Then came 20 years of uncertainty about whether the place would disappear. Finally, in 2010, building permission came through.

In April 2013, it was relaunched as Le Louxor – Palais du cinéma. After catching a movie, go have a drink on the sublime terrace looking out over the boulevard.

Address 170 Boulevard Magenta, 75010 Paris, +33 (0)1 44 63 96 98 | Getting there Metro to Barbès-Rochechouart (Lines 2 and 4) | Tip More of Egypt in Paris can be found at 2 Place du Caire: the façade of the building is decorated with three heads of the goddess Hathor, representing love, joy, and music and dance. And at the exit of the Vaneau Metro station, at 42 Rue de Sèvres, an Egyptian water carrier stands guard, a jug in each hand.

65 Les Magasins Crespin-Dufayel

The glory days of commerce

There is nothing like a good old-fashioned department store building to stoke your sense of theatricality.

In 1856, a big department store opened under the name of *Palais de la Nouveauté* (Palace of Novelties) on the east of the Butte Montmartre, at 26 Rue de Clignancourt. Its director was Jacques-François Crespin, a farmer's son, and his shop specialized in selling goods on installment plans – from furniture and household goods to jewelry and clothing. Its motto? "Work. Credit. Confidence."

After Crespin died in 1888, Georges Dufayel, who'd worked under Crespin since 1871, took over the Palais de la Nouveauté. At its height in 1910, it was the most important department store in Europe, taking up a hectare of space and employing 15,000 people! The various boutiques were connected by two railway tracks, and from deliveries for all over France departed from the stables each day. Dufayel wasn't content to make sales; he also wanted to keep his clients coming back for more, which inspired him to create a conservatory garden and a theater on premises.

The Crespin-Dufayel department stores were decked out in an incredible rococo style. A splendid curving staircase wound from the ground floor to the upper stories. More than two hundred statues decorated the interior and the façade, the latter of which still looks as it did back then. The pediment that sits atop the building was made in 1892 by Jules Dalou and is adorned with sculptures by Alexandre Falguière, depicting allegorical figures of Progress, Commerce, and Industry. There is a whole story going on up there, crowned by a big dome, on top of which there was formerly an electric lamplight that lit up the entryways. The place was closed in 1930 and BNP took over the building after World War II.

Address 26 Rue de Clignancourt, 75018 Paris | Getting there Metro to Château Rouge
(Line 4) | Tip The Zara boutique, at the corner of 140 Rue de Rennes and Rue Blaise-
Desgoffe, occupies the building of one of the first Félix Potin stores in Paris – one of the
biggest commercial successes of the past century. Take a good look at the corner turret and
you will see, written in gold, the name of Félix Potin.

66 __ Le Magic Mirror
A magical marvel

Are you aching to get in touch with your inner child? Head to Musée des Arts Forains, which is filled with treasures collected over many years by Jean-Paul Favand. If you take the guided tour, which lasts an hour and a half, you will be led through all of these marvels: carousels, shooting ranges, parading gondolas. And it is all very hands on – you can climb onto the carousel horses, hop into the gondolas, and touch all of the objects on display. Kids love it there, but so do adults – it is like a trip back in time. You will feel like a royal from the 19th century in Little Venice, as background music plays Mady Mesplé taking on the best of Italian arias, from Monteverdi to Verdi. The shadow-theater shows at night bring back figures like Jules Verne's Captain Nemo and Sarah Bernhardt.

Of all these rooms installed in the old wine cellars of Bercy, the Magic Mirror is one of the most... magical! You will have to show ID to get inside, and it is only open on the *Journées du Patrimoine* holidays or during Festival du Merveilleux. This superb mahogany-covered "travelling ballroom" from the 1920s is equipped with a dance floor in the middle and is surrounded by twelve private boxes that add a little intimacy to the place. Back in the day, the Magic Mirror moved around all over the place before planting its bigtop tent in the middle of the old wine cellars near the Théâtre de Verdure. Also called "the tent of mirrors," it is the only original Magic Mirror ballroom that still exists in France. It is made of a wooden structure decked out in hundreds of beveled mirrors, an elegy to the talent of mirror makers of yore, who were the first to play with optical illusions and the special effects of light reflection. You can also rent the Magic Mirror for a special occasion. In dressing up for the event, you will feel like you're in a time machine headed straight back to *les Années Folles*!

Address 53 Avenue des Terroirs-de-France, 75012 Paris, +33 (0)1 43 40 16 15, www.artsforains.com | **Getting there** Metro to Cour Saint-Émilion (Line 14) | **Hours** One-and-a-half-hour guided visits all year long; museum open on school holidays; the Magic Mirror is open for the *Journées du Patrimoine* holidays and during Festival du Merveilleux, from Christmas to the beginning of January. | **Tip** Whether you already have a green thumb or not, the Maison du Jardinage, free and open to everyone, housed right in the middle of the Parc du Bercy, will teach you all the tricks of the trade. A library is even at the disposal of any horticulture enthusiasts (+33 (0)1 53 46 19 19).

67__Maison Plisson

Gourmet groceries

This newish spot on Boulevard Beaumarchais has been packed since opening its doors in 2015. I was actually there when it opened: there was a line down the sidewalk to get a table on the terrace.

How do you go from being at the helm of Claudie Pierlot clothing line to a running a hit restaurant-boutique? Apparently without a hitch, says Delphine Plisson, the owner of this wildly popular spot. But it should be said that Plisson has the energy to move mountains. After three years spent running around France hunting down the best local products, the result is top notch.

As soon as you enter Maison Plisson, you will think you are back in the time of Les Halles. You will feel like you're in the Billy Wilder movie *Irma la Douce*. The sellers wear old-fashioned blue aprons and offer samples of all the gourmet products displayed on the counters: charcuterie, cheeses known and unknown, seasonal produce.

On the ground floor, to the right, you can shop for farm-fresh produce; on the left, you can sit down in the dining room, which is meant to make you feel like you are eating in someone's home. With its 120 tables, half of which are on the terrace, the place was designed to be able to prepare on premises all the products sold in the boutique.

In the basement, you will find everything your pantry could ask for: cookies, jams, oils, gourmet spreads – 45 of them were tested all over the country in order to offer the very best! – and over 300 wines.

Maison Plisson has two famous backers: Yves Camdeborde (of Le Comptoir and L'Avant-Comptoir, on the Relais Saint-Germain) and Bruno Doucet of La Régalade, in the 14th arrondissement. Camborde's famous *riz au lait* is served there, and the baked goods are taken care of by Benoît Castel (see ch. 61), and made right before your eyes.

Not everything is perfect, but it is very good, and served with a smile in spite of the crowds.

Address 93 Boulevard Beaumarchais, 75011 Paris, www.lamaisonplisson.com | **Getting there** Metro to Saint-Sébastien – Froissart (Line 8) | **Hours** Mon – Sat 8:30am – 9pm; Sun 8:30am – 5pm | **Tip** If Maison Plisson is full, do not panic – a nearby food truck is there to save the day. Le Réfectoire is in the 11th arrondissement twice a week. On the menu: burgers and hot dogs with artisanal buns, *viande française* and fries. What's more, the six different burger options can all be made with vegetarian patties (Tuesday and Friday, 107 Boulevard Richard Lenoir).

68 Maison Souquet

A brothel-turned-hotel

Apart from the two red streetlights, there is no sign that this hotel is a former brothel. But as soon as you enter the vestibule, a strange atmosphere sinks in: first by its sumptuous perfume of rose and jasmine, then by its oriental décor – the voluptuous sofas in deep red are so inviting.

Baudelaire wrote in his famous *Invitation au voyage*: "My child, my sister, think how sweet to go out and live there together…" The lines of the poem seem like a definite influence on the hotel's owners, Sylviane Sanz and Yoni Aidan.

If it was not poetry that inspired the décor, however, it has to have been the scandalous past of this house of pleasure, which was run by a certain Madame Souquet from 1905 to 1907 after having previously been a school for young girls. Located in the middle of Pigalle, two steps from the Moulin Rouge, the hotel has bet everything on this sultry thematic: they bargain-hunted the furniture, which dates from the early 20th century, and brought back magnificent enamel paneling, copper-plated in the Moorish style and dating from 1895, from Brussels. It took three months just to install them onto the walls of the *salon des mille et une nuits*.

Jacques Garcia, a hot Parisian decorator, used no fewer than 120 different fabrics in the three living rooms and the 20-odd bedrooms, which are all named after courtesans and mistresses (La Païva, La Belle Otero, La Castiglione, e.g.). For those world travelers accustomed to luxury, a spa with a 33-foot-long pool is available one hour a day for private use. My dream! But for now I will content myself with hanging out in the *salon d'hiver* to try out a delicate tea chosen by the master Tseng, or maybe I will head to the *salon des petits bonheurs* to sip a mysterious cocktail under the 12 lustrous glass figurines of female bodies and the 84 heads of grimacing satyr sculptures in the paneling.

Address 10 Rue de Bruxelles, 75009 Paris, +33 (0)1 48 78 55 55, www.maisonsouquet.com | Getting there Metro to Blanche (Line 2) | Hours Bar-restaurant until 1am | Tip Take in a bit of greenery in the Adolphe-Max Square, where Édouard Vuillard had his atelier at number 6. In the middle, a statue of Hector Berlioz reminds you that the musician died right nearby, in 1869, at 4 Rue de Calais.

69__Le Manoir de Paris

For nerves of steel

I wasn't scared, I swear! Not a bit. I didn't scream, didn't beg, I didn't even close my eyes waiting in line for the Manoir de Paris! On the contrary, I kept them wide open to admire the splendid ceramic frescoes that adorn the place. Because this beautiful building, landmarked as an historical monument in 1981, was once the headquarters of Faïenceries Boulenger de Choisy-le-Roi, a tile manufacturer. One of the walls of the façade of the building has been redone in their famous white beveled tile.

Today the Manoir de Paris is home to the first haunted-house show in France. It was the brainchild of a young American named Adil Houti, who first tried out the concept in Texas. The house stages 17 Parisian legends that take place in spooky settings like the catacombs, the sewers, the Metro, and the Père-Lachaise cemetery. Each level up gets scarier and scarier until you reach the asylum, the grimmest floor of all.

As you wait in line to get in, you will have to divide yourself into groups of four people. After a quick "Bon courage!" you are off, weaving in and out of barely lit corridors. "I'm scared of the dark!" shrieked one young girl in my group – and yet, it was her third time visiting the place.

As you wade through the darkness, you will be shouted at by strange characters – young actors incarnating witches, hunchbacks, or blood-covered butchers – who jump out from behind curtains or from the murky darkness of a torture room. Their goal is simple: to scare the wits out of you. But don't worry, at the end this long path of total darkness, you will emerge unscathed. Claustrophobes or those with heart problems are not allowed; neither are pregnant women, "sensitive" people, or children under 12 years. According to my secret sources, Halloween is the scariest of the shows! The girls in my group were determined to come back again soon. "We're addicted!"

Address 18 Rue de Paradis, 75010 Paris | Getting there Metro to Château d'Eau (Line 4) or Poissonnière (Line 7), or RER to Gare de l'Est | Hours Afternoons until 10pm. Reservations at www.lemanoirdeparis.fr | Tip You must see the magnificent Françoise-Sagan media library at 8 Rue Léon-Schwartzenberg, in the Carré Saint-Lazare, an historic site dating from the 12th century. Closed Sundays and Mondays, you can find the hours at www.equipement.paris.fr/mediatheque-francoise-sagan-8695L.

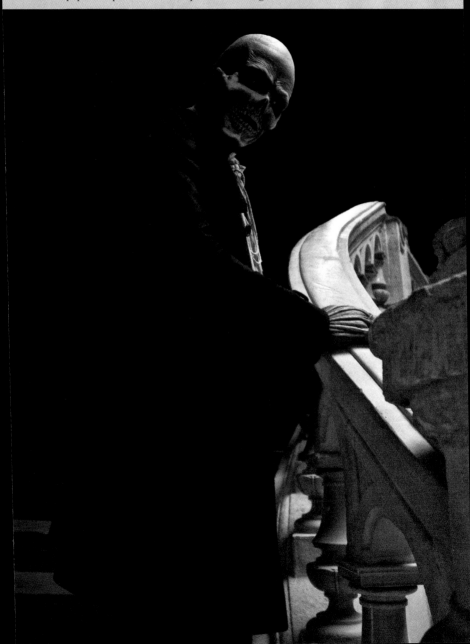

70__La Manufacture 111

The beat of the city

If you happen to be searching for a place that brings together all different kinds of urban experiences, look no further – I have found the place. It is called La Manufacture 111, and it is housed in a giant space converted into a 5,000-square-foot loft, with a 250-square-foot gallery, an auditorium, a bar-restaurant and – very soon – a terrace, to boot!

The place is basically a multifaceted temple in honor of street-culture. It is teeming with projects and collective performances, with young contemporary artists invited to create works or experimental installations, like the ones in 2015 from the Berlin artist Clemens Behr. Certain artists have opted for the comical route, like Jean-Claude Muaka and his show called *One Man Costaud*, or Hervé Dipari, the winner of the Tremplin Humour in 2015. At Manufacture 111, artists are not meant to be abstract, inaccessible figures, but people you can go right up and talk to.

In the auditorium, awesome projections will plunge you into the universe of freestyle, show you unseen works by the street artist Banksy, teach you about the history of hip-hop, or the life and works of Jean-Michel Basquiat.

Music groups and DJs are regularly invited, making the (rather thick) walls reverberate with good music and lots of energy. At the bar-restaurant, you can either have a drink, or settle down to do a bit of work alone or with friends. The concept store Dernier-Né will show you the latest works from young designers – Billie Sacré-Coeur, De Paris Yearbook, Metropolitan, Misericordia, Vague & Lame. The place also boasts a shelf of records and a bookstore, with a well-curated selection of works on contemporary art.

On Thursday nights, you can see live shows by an artist who creates works right before your eyes! And every Sunday, Manufacture offers a themed brunch – one week it is African, another week Moroccan, and another week Asian.

Address 19 Boulevard Davout, 75020 Paris, +33 (0)1 40 33 01 36, www.manufacture111.com | **Getting there** Metro to Porte de Vincennes (Line 1) | **Hours** Tues–Sat 1pm–8pm (Thu until 10pm), Sun 10am–8pm | **Tip** If after bathing yourself in street culture, you're dying to eat a good, proper meal in a super bourgeois setting, try out Allobroges (71 Rue des Grands-Champs, +33 (0)1 43 73 40 00, Metro to Maraîchers (Line 9), closed Sun).

71__The Marais Dance Center

From stagecoaches to dance classes

At the Hôtel de Berlize, my tap dance class is held in the Mozart room. Musicality, coordination, memory, perseverance, and a certain "cool" are required to make progress. But I'll have to leave all that up to Martine Raveaux. Like other instructors at the Centre de danse du Marais (The Marais Dance Center), she's a seasoned professional. This school is, above all, a reservoir of talent, filled with high-level performers from all over the world who come to hone their skills in flamenco, salsa, ballet, contemporary, Indian dance, Balinese, and Oriental.

Sixty disciplines are taught throughout the year – the biggest variety you can find in Paris – and it is located right in the historic heart of the Marais. In the 19th century, it was a coaching inn called l'Auberge de l'Aigle d'Or (Inn of the Golden Eagle). The garden and the courtyard, covered by a wooden framework, were set up to accept deliveries by stagecoaches. In 1920, the place was saved from demolition when it was designated a historical landmark.

Antoine Carrance, the owner of the dance center, tells how this place came into being through his family. In 1930, his grandfather bought the place after falling in love with the paved courtyard and the buildings surrounding it. In the 1960s, Micheline, Antoine's mother, a pharmacist by trade and a passionate dancer, transformed the beautiful salons into dance studios and created the center. In 1970, they removed the shed in the courtyard and rebuilt a structure in the back to house the seating area of the Café de la Gare, the famous café-theater started by the comedian Coluche and his friends. Meanwhile, the tiny Théâtre Essaïon is nestled in the cellars. A restaurant and a terrace have now settled into the courtyard. Over the years, the reputation of the dance center has grown and the old walls of the Hôtel de Berlize are always buzzing with activity.

Address 41 Rue du Temple, 75004 Paris, +33 (0)1 42 88 58 19, www.paris-danse.com |
Getting there Metro to Hôtel de Ville (Line 1 and 11) | Hours Every day 9:30am–10pm |
Tip Le Perchoir Marais, the bar on the terrace of the BHV Marais, is blessed with an
unobstructed view of the rooftops (37 Rue de la Verrerie, every day 10:15pm–2am, except
Wed 9:15pm–2am and Sun 12:30pm–2am).

72 __ The Marché sur l'eau

A market on a boat for the eco-minded

Who wouldn't want to find produce as fresh as if they were in the countryside? Well, Marché sur l'eau has it! With subscription to the market costing an average of 10€ a year, it gives you access to local fruits and vegetables, Bries, goat cheeses, farm eggs, honey collected in Île-de-France, and lots more. The subscriber model lets the producers harvest only what will be consumed, while allowing the consumer to discover original products – for example long-forgotten vegetables like gold ball turnips and oxheart cabbage.

The Marché sur l'eau association was founded in 2012 to promote locavore produce, which is more environmentally responsible. Every Tuesday and Saturday, an old oyster-farming boat leaves Meaux, about 30 miles from Paris, and goes up the Marne and the Canal de l'Ourcq to reach Pantin four hours later, just in time to deliver weekly basket of produce to subscribers. The Marché sur l'eau also offers a retail market for non-subscribers who prefer to make their purchases depending on what is offered. The deliveries to Paris are made using a biogas-powered truck. The sellers set up stalls in a tree-lined space at the foot of the Rotonde de Ledoux, across from the Bassin de la Villette. The business model works thanks to the employees of the association, but also thanks to the volunteers who take care of loading and unloading the boat and truck.

You can either order your basket online and pick it up at a specified location, or shop for goods directly from the members of the association on the days of the market. The selection is varied: organic vegetables from Meaux or Changis-sur-Marne, asparagus from Verdelot, lentils, grains, and hazelnuts from Crécy-la-Chapelle, apples from the Pomamour orchard in Gressy, near Claye-Souilly, just to name a few. Marché sur l'eau also publishes recipes based on the harvest on their website.

Address 6-8 Place de La Bataille-de-Stalingrad, in front of La Rotonde, 75019 Paris; 28 Quai de l'Aisne (under the walkway facing Feeling Dance Factory), 93500 Pantin, www.marchesurleau.com | Getting there Metro to Stalingrad or Jaurès (Lines 2, 5, and 7bis); or RER to Pantin (Line E) | Hours Tue 6pm–8pm (basket pick-up); Sat 11:30am–1:30pm (basket and retail market); Sat noon–2pm (Pantin retail market) | Tip It is worth grabbing brunch, a drink, or a bite at La Rotonde, the brasserie under the magnificent rotunda (+33 (0)1 80 48 33 40).

73__Marie Bashkirtseff's Grave

In honor of a short life

It is impossible to miss it: built as an orthodox chapel, topped with a dome and a pinnacle, the grave of Marie Bashkirtseff is the biggest and tallest of this cemetery that sprawls above the Place du Trocadero. Anyone who was anyone in French high society is buried here, from the writer Jean Giraudoux to Georges Mandel, the politician assassinated in 1944; from Édouard Manet to his sister-in-law Berthe Morisot. Along the promenade, you will find musicians like Gabriel Fauré, Claude Debussy, and also pass by Henry Farman, one of the pioneers of aviation.

Life is short. And it was very short for Marie Bashkirtseff, a young woman remembered for the diary she kept from the age of 14 until her death by tuberculosis 12 years later. Born in 1858 in Ukraine, she spoke several languages fluently and was a passionate student of the Classical world. She moved to France as a young girl with her mother, and decided to become a painter at a time when art school was for men only.

She got into the Académie Julian, the only school that accepted women. The Musée d'Orsay has one of her works, titled *Un meeting*, which was shown at the Salon de 1884. The naturalist painting enjoyed a small success, as did several of her portraits. Her diary tracks her commitment to art and her obsession with the idea of making her mark. "But what do I want? Oh! You know very well. I want glory! And it is not this diary that will give it to me. This diary won't be published until after my death, for I'm too naked here to reveal while I'm still alive. It will be but the complement of an illustrious life." Alas, death took her soon – in Paris, October 1884 – and it is indeed her diary by which she is remembered. Though if you stick your nose up to the window of the monument's door, you can spot the last canvas completed by the artist, *Les saintes femmes au tombeau.*

Address Cimetière de Passy, 2 Rue du Commandant-Schloesing, 75016 Paris, +33 (0)1 53 70 40 80 | Getting there Metro to Trocadéro (Lines 6 and 9) | Hours Mon–Fri 8am–5:30pm; Sat 8:30am–5:30pm; Sun 9am–5:30pm | Tip Among the celebrities resting in the Passy cemetery, there's Fernandel, one of the most popular French actors, who died in 1971, and whose grave is always covered in flowers.

74 _ The Maubuée Fountain

The oldest fountain in Paris

At the top of the Centre Georges-Pompidou square, the oldest fountain in Paris peeks out, oh-so-discreetly, just waiting to catch the eye of the most observant passersby. Will you notice this testament to the daily life of Paris, half-buried as it is into the urban landscape? Not as easy as you might think, as the evolution of the city often hides its traces: vestiges of the past rub shoulders with contemporary architecture, and sometimes it is hard when you see them all together to distinguish the seductive colors of Beaubourg.

But once you manage to find the fountain, its charm is guaranteed to win you over. Its stones are so worn by the passing of centuries that they have taken on the softness of a vase filled with aquatic flowers. Its name, however, is somewhat less overtly seductive. *Maubuée* means "bad laundry," which was meant to be taken to heart as a comment on the quality of the water – too limy to be used for washing your linens! Displaced by the construction of the Centre Georges Pompidou, the fountain in its present state dates from the 18th century, but the original, before its reconstruction, dates back to the 13th century.

In the past, fountains were above all functional and completely necessary: they were the meeting places for the distribution of water. In Paris, water has always been a fundamental issue. The ever-increasing number of inhabitants made its consumption and distribution a serious matter. Fed by the trickling underground waters, captured on the heights of Belleville and Ménilmontant, these fountains just were not enough to quench everyone's needs. Meanwhile, the water from the Seine made people sick. It was not until the Napoleonic Empire that, thanks to the canalization from the Ourcq River to the Villette Reservoir, Paris succeeded in getting enough clean water into the city to satisfy the needs of all Parisians.

Address At the corner of Rue Saint-Martin and Rue de Venise, 75004 Paris | Getting there Metro to Rambuteau (Line 11) | Tip A little further, you will find one of the most beautiful fountains in Paris: the Stravinsky Fountain, where colorful creations by Niki de Saint Phalle, and more "mechanical" ones by Jean Tinguely, pay tribute to the famous Russian composer.

75___The Momboye Dance Center

African rhythms

Paris is a city that moves and a city open to the world! Most notably to Africa, in all its diversity, which occupies an important place in France. And exploring its cultures of dance might be the best way to discover it without leaving the capital. The Centre Momboye is the perfect address to let yourself go to the beat of African rhythms.

Georges Momboye is a choreographer of Ivorian origin who, fluent in African dances since childhood, went on to train with the best in ballet, jazz, and contemporary dance. In his own work, he incorporates African dances into contemporary forms to create a choreographic language that is completely unique.

Tapped by UNESCO to create his first choreographic work, he formed his company in 1992, which presents new works every year on international tours. The dance center followed in 1998. The desire to pass on his knowledge and to teach African dance styles was important for Georges Momboye, but it was inconceivable for him to do so without being accompanied by live traditional music.

The challenge then was to find a spot in Paris that could host African percussion at all hours without getting complaints from neighbors. You will notice yourself that the center only has one wall attached to a neighboring building. Georges Momboye also surrounds himself with the best teachers from the world of dance. The 40-plus faculty members hail from all different disciplines to highlight the diversity of different African dance techniques and to create an opening for other dances marked by African influence. The center offers weekly classes and weekend workshops in dance traditions from Cameroon, Mali, Congo, Guinea, and Senegal, not to mention Afro-Brazilian, Capoeira, salsa, Argentine tango, raga, and kizomba. There's practically the whole world to choose from!

Address 25 Rue Boyer, 75020 Paris, +33 (0)1 43 58 85 01, www.centre-momboye.com | Getting there Metro to Ménilmontant (Line 2) or Pelleport (Line 3bis) | Hours Check website for class schedule, Mon–Fri 7pm–10pm; Sat & Sun 10am–6pm | Tip If a few hours of African dance works up your appetite, the center is located right next to La Bellevilloise, the capital's first cooperative from 1887. It reopened in 2005 as a restaurant and concert hall.

76__Notre-Dame de la Médaille Miraculeuse

A pilgrimage to Paris

Almost thirty years before the miracle at Lourdes, Paris hosted its own series of apparitions of the Virgin Mary. The place where it happened is now a site of pilgrimage for Catholics of all nationalities. But no matter your faith, or whether you're a believer or not, it is absolutely captivating to visit this chapel – if only to witness the stark contrast between the devotion within and the buzzing ambiance of the capital outside its walls.

In 1830, the Virgin Mary appeared here three times to a 24-year-old nun, Soeur Catherine Labouré, who'd joined the religious order of *les Filles de la Charité de Saint Vincent de Paul* that same year. The apparitions took place in the sanctuary of the chapel, which at the time was dedicated to the Sacred Heart of Jesus. The current chapel dates from the 1930s and the blue and gold mosaics in its interior tell the story of the visions of the Saint Catherine (who was canonized in 1947).

After appearing to reveal the young girl's divine mission, the Virgin Mary explained all the project's details during a second appearance. Catherine had a vision of a medal emblazoned with a prayer that the Virgin told her to have minted and distributed to those wishing to receive her good graces. The medal has been minted since 1832, when Paris was facing a terrible epidemic of cholera. The recoveries achieved after the medal's distribution led Parisians to call it "miraculous," and the chapel became a popular site of pilgrimage.

The story spread across the Catholic world, and today this miraculous medal draws more than two million pilgrims annually. In spite of the constant comings and goings, an air of contemplation reigns in this chapel situated in the heart of the very commercial Bon Marché neighborhood.

Address 140 Rue du Bac, 75007 Paris, +33 (0)1 49 54 78 88, www.chappellenotredamedelamedaillemiraculeuse.com | **Getting there** Metro to Rue du Bac (Line 12) | **Hours** Every day, 7:45am–1pm and 2:30pm–7pm; all day on Tuesdays. | **Tip** On leaving, in the alley leading to the chapel, you will notice the statue of Saint-Vincent-de-Paul, founder of the order of Sainte-Catherine-Labouré. If you like the idea of discovering another small little-known chapel, know that this one welcoming relics of the saint can be found just nearby, at 95 Rue des Sèvres.

77 _Notre-Dame-du-Travail

The faith of the working class

Behind the ensemble of buildings designed in 1985 by the Catalan architect Ricardo Bofill, you will find one of the most unique churches in the capital.

At first glance, nothing really looks all that special about it. From the outside, it is a religious building like any other, albeit with somewhat imposing dimensions. The surprising element is found on the inside, which looks like the interior of a factory! The nave is entirely made out of metal: 135 tons of iron and steel.

In the second half of the 19th century, the *Expositions universelles* were growing at a rapid pace, requiring the labor of hundreds of factory workers. They lived for the most part in the housing projects that had sprung up in the Plaisance area of the 14th arrondissement. But there was only one small chapel for the faithful, located on what is now Rue du Texel. In 1886, when the Abbot Soulange-Bodin was named vicar of Plaisance, he decided a new place of worship was needed: "Whom is a church for? To unite laborers of all classes. Why in Paris? Because Paris is rightly considered the center of labor and of industry. Why in the Plaisance neighborhood? Because it is a district composed solely of laborers, which does not yet have a church for its 35,000 dwellers, but which is admirably prepared to obtain one, with its remarkable ensemble of religious and social works."

Notre-Dame-du-Travail (Our Lady of Labor) was created to make its factory-worker worshippers feel right at home – that is, at work. In all its austerity, the church's extraordinary nave manages to maintain a certain lightness, thanks to the thin iron columns supporting its vaults. These columns came from the Palais de l'Industrie, which was constructed for the *Exposition universelle* of 1885. The walls and the sacristy are adorned with paintings, plants, and flowers. The clock above was taken from Sebastopol in 1854 by Napoléon III.

Address 59 Rue Vercingétorix, 75014, Paris, +33 (0)1 44 10 72 92, www.notredamedutravail.net | Getting there Metro to Pernety (Line 13) | Hours Mon–Fri 7:30am–7:45pm; Sat 8:45am–7:45pm; Sun 8:45am–7:30pm | Tip You should also go see the building in the Allée du Château-Ouvrier at 69 Rue Raymond-Losserand. Built in 1891, the units in this stone-and-brick rental building had toilets in their apartments – a huge luxury at the time! It almost disappeared at the end of the 1980s, but was saved thanks to the fight put up by its last occupants and neighbors.

78_ L'Oasis d'Aboukir

The plant man strikes again

This gorgeous green wall is located in the Sentier neighborhood, a dense, frantic, and very urban area known for its textiles.

At the corner of Rue d'Aboukir and Rue des Petits-Carreaux, an enormous wall of greenery has been up since 2013. It is yet another creation by the botanical artist Patrick Blanc, who has already deployed his talents at the Cité des Sciences et de l'Industrie and at the Musée du quai Branly. He's the one who invented these green walls, and he's worked with some big shots on them: André Putman, Jean Nouvel, and Renzo Piano. He even covered an entire 500-foot-high tower in Sydney with plants. At the Pérez Art Museum Miami, he put up 70 "greenified" columns.

Funded by a private initiative, this project in the middle of Paris was perfectly suited to Blanc, who loves introducing biodiversity onto city walls. What's more, vertical vegetation allows horizontal space to be left to urban activities. On a surface area of 2,700 feet and measuring 80 feet high, he planted 7,600 plants and 237 different species of shrubs. All of which have grown "like mushrooms," as they say in French.

Standing at the foot of the Oasis d'Aboukir is absolutely breathtaking. It is entirely covered in very dense plant life, which seems to have no problem attaching itself to the wall. Blanc's process is simple: he fastens a wet cloth to a plastic board. Then he chooses the plants depending on their position. Those that are high up and are more exposed to sunlight form a canopy; those on the bottom stay in the shade. At first glance, the green wall looks just like, well, a green wall. But upon further inspection, you will start to distinguish all the different plants and flowers in all their varying shades. As the wall is oriented to the southwest, the plants flower a lot. For the best view of the Oasis, take a seat right across from it on the low wall.

Address Corner of Rue d'Aboukir and Rue des Petits-Carreaux, 75002 Paris | **Getting there** Metro to Sentier (Line 3) | **Tip** At any hour of the day (and almost any hour of the night!), you can go down and check out Tambour, a "bucolic urban bistro," with its old wooden Metro bench seating, its antique Parisian street signs and bus stops, and its colorful regulars (41 Rue Montmartre, 2nd arrondissement, +33 (0)1 42 33 06 90).

79__ The Owls

Rise above

This sublime space in the Haut Marais used to go by the name of Café Rouge, but since the Fall of 2015, it has had a new look thanks the Catalan architect talent Lázaro Rosa-Violán, whose art-deco-ish revamp is stunning. The place is enormous: a white painted-metal structure – very Gustave Eiffel – divides three wrap-around stories of dining areas centered around a vast patio, and crowned by a wall of windows twenty meters high. The upper levels are passageways, into which are tucked several private rooms where you can dine, or maybe just curl up in an armchair to read next to a magnificent chimney of enameled lava. The restaurant seems to want to feed your soul as much as it does your body. Those who prefer a more social scene are invited to sit at the (rather majestic) communal table, just below the wall of enormous windows.

The menu changes twice a month, offering a choice between three *entrées*, three *plats*, and three desserts. A great selection of wine is housed in a beautiful armoire with glass doors – you feel like you are at a library. My meal was excellent: a cod confit with cream of beans and Serrano pepper, and one of my favorite desserts, a Paris-Brest *croustillant noisette* pastry.

Les Chouettes is equally known for its *eaux de vie* from the Stählemühle; some people come specifically for tastings.

It is located right at the site of the Enclos du Temple. In the Middle Ages, one part of the Knights Templar order installed itself here after returning from the siege of Saint-Jean-d'Arc in 1291. In 1312, the order, which served as the creditor to the king, was dissolved and had its goods confiscated by Philippe IV, who was jealous of its power. Just behind Les Chouettes, at 73 Rue Charlot, parallel to the Rue de Picardie, is one of the only remaining vestiges of the Enclos du Temple: a tower that has been integrated into the offices of company now occupying the building.

Address 32 Rue de Picardie, 75003 Paris, +33 (0)1 44 61 73 21 | **Getting there** Metro to Filles du Calvaire (Line 8) | **Hours** Every day 8:30am–1am | **Tip** If you are curious to see what the Enclos du Temple looked like a long time ago, check out the basement of Carreau du Temple, where there's a model replica. This will give you the chance to discover that magnificent metallic *halle*, once used as a second-hand clothes store, which has been transformed into a very popular interdisciplinary cultural center (4 Rue Eugène-Spuller, www.carreaudutemple.eu).

80_Paris-Gobelins Station
A station disappears

South of the 13th arrondissement, you can spot the old Gobelins train station from three different standpoints: from the top of the Tokyo tower built perpendicularly above it; from the bridge on Rue Regnault that crosses the rail tracks next to Rue Nationale; or next to the plaza taken over by skaters. This unusual spot, emerging as it does from the depths of the city, was the terminal of a now-abandoned circle line that linked Paris' main railway stations. It was the location of a freight train station created by the city of Paris in 1903 that allowed goods to be delivered directly to nearby factories, including the Say sugar refinery and the Maison-Blanche natural gas factory. Of those old structures of the industrial past of yore, the only one still standing is the Panhard-Levassor factory, which was the beating heart of the automobile industry.

In the 1970s, one of the largest Parisian construction sites led to the creation of the Olympiades neighborhood. The freight station was covered over by a plaza, huge underground spaces were laid out beneath, and a shopping center and high-rise buildings were built – all named for cities that had hosted Olympic Games. On the plaza, a shopping mall composed of pagodas offers a rare sight – you would think you were in Asia.

The Gobelins train station was in operation until 1991, after which freight trains were banned from the line circling Paris. Only two bits of platforms with rails and some grass-covered switch stations remain. A stretch of asphalt is used as a parking lot for trucks that make deliveries to the supermarkets on Avenue d'Ivry. Homeless people seek shelter in the tunnel that links the station to the Petite Ceinture (the line that circles Paris) – they are known as the *tunnelois*. Under the plaza, the rail tracks have been replaced by Rue Javelot and Rue du Disque, whose names also make reference to the Olympics.

Address Near Square Ulysse-Trélat, 112 Rue Régnault, 75013 Paris | Getting there Metro (Line 7) or tramway (Line T3a) to Porte d'Ivry | Tip Near 34 Rue Nationale, do not miss Passage Bourgoin, the only surviving mini-street from the old days, with its little artisan-built houses from around 1880.

81 Passage de la Sorcière
The witch is in prison!

I have to tell you a secret – I love going up and down the stairs of Paris, and particularly the ones in Montmartre! That is why a few years ago my friend Anna Rychkoff, a sidewalk portrait artist, took me to one of the neighborhood's steep hills and showed me her favorite secret staircase.

And secret for a good reason! It is found in the Passage de la Sorcière, which is currently closed to the public. But I could not resist the urge to reveal it to you, along with two tips to get past the door codes. You can either cozy up to a boule-playing member of the private club, which makes use of the most discreet pétanque court in the city, or you can reserve a table at Hôtel Particulier Montmartre, the chic establishment with a topnotch restaurant.

Going up the staircase from Rue Lepic, the strange mass sitting right in the middle might catch you off guard. It is actually a famous boulder called the Rocher de la Sorcière, or the witch's rock. Rumors have been circulating about it forever. According to geologists, the rock came from La Marne, near Reims. Other more fantastically inclined scientists have made conjectures about it being a meteorite! What is most likely is that the boulder is a vestige of a former spring water fountain, in this passage "of the witch." Its name came into being thanks to a bunch of hoodlums who yelled the epithet at some poor lady living in the passage.

Today it is a verdant path, surrounded by the last shrubs of the former scrublands of Montmartre. And apparently it is quite conducive to romance – they say that lovers who touch the rock are protected by the witch. At the very least, it has provoked fierce arguments in the neighborhood since its closing in June 2009. Some residents have rallied to have it reopened with a petition called "Free the Witch" (*Libérez la Sorcière*). But as of now she's still locked up behind bars.

Address 65 Rue Lepic and 23 Avenue Junot, 75018 Paris | **Getting there** Metro to Abbesses (Line 12) | **Tip** At 54 Rue Lepic, you will find the house of Théo Van Gogh, Vincent's brother. A plaque explains that he lived here from 1886 to 1888.

82 Passerelle d'Aubervilliers
Paris towards the millennium!

Paris changes. It transforms. The capital is currently taking measures to better link the city to its surrounding suburbs with the help of footbridges. Since October 1, 2015, a particularly fantastic *passerelle* in the shape of an arc was installed to connect the Claude-Bernard ZAC urban development project in the 19th arrondissement to the Millénaire commercial center in the north-eastern suburb of Aubervilliers. Covered in wooden panels, about 330 feet long and 13 feet wide, the sloping footbridge allows pedestrians, strollers, and bicycles to avoid detours and pass directly from one neighborhood to the other. Before its creation, they had to go through the Porte d'Aubervilliers.

Between the Périphérique highway and the Canal Saint-Denis, several Department of Justice services are located in the Millénaire 3, an imposing glass building of 32,000 square meters linking the Porte de la Villette and the Porte d'Aubervilliers. Other similar projects are on their way.

The 2012 extension of the T3 tramway line was a game-changer for this formerly disadvantaged neighborhood. It goes through the center of the enormous group of buildings occupying what was once a merchandise warehouse on the Boulevard Macdonald. That is 1.8 million square feet reimagined as a multifaceted space to suit the needs of a city. It includes 1,200 housing units, some of these were constructed by the architect Mathieu Mercuriali directly on the roof of the old warehouse! There's also 325,000 square feet of office space, 480,000 square feet of activity space (150 start-ups have just set up shop), businesses, and equipment available to the public for research and sports. From 118 to 166 Boulevard Macdonald, new buildings keep popping up in this immense eco-neighborhood. The banks of the Canal Saint-Denis were brought to make the promenade. Check it out, then take the footbridge to Aubervilliers!

Address Passerelle along the Rue Lounès-Matoub, 75019 Paris | Getting there Metro to Porte de la Villette (Line 7) | Tip In the south of Paris, in the 14th arrondissement, you can also cross over the Périphérique highway by foot. From the Parc de la Cité Universitaire Internationale, in front of the Église du Sacré-Cœur de Gentilly, the footbridge called the Passerelle du Cambodge carries pedestrians and cyclists all the way to Avenue Paul-Vaillant-Couturier in Gentilly. 2017 heralds the year this somewhat shabby footbridge will be touched up to look a little snappier.

83_Passerelle Debilly

The crime scene

Was it a case of spying? Sexual assault? On January 4, 1988, between 2:00 and 3:00 in the morning, Siegfried Wielsputz, 31 years old, was beaten on the Passerelle Debilly footbridge. This German citizen and member of the Secret Services was responsible for the legal services at the German Consulate. In his pocket, investigators found a pamphlet from the ERNK (National Liberation Front of Kurdistan). For the year that followed, tensions soared between ERNK militants and German authorities, who suspected Kurdish militants were responsible for attacks taking place on Turks in Germany.

But the Kurds fought back against these accusations. Was it possible to envision another hypothesis linked to the homosexuality of the victim? The crime has remained unsolved since 1988. Whatever happened, it has the makings of a good movie, and in fact, the Passerelle Debilly has already appeared in films – *La Fille sur le pont*, for example, a 1999 film by Patrice Leconte with Vanessa Paradis and Daniel Auteuil.

The footbridge was named for the general of Billy (which became Debilly), who was killed in October 1806 during the *Bataille d'Iéna*, which marked the victory of Napoleon's troops over the Prussians.

It was built for the spectacular World Fair of 1900, which welcomed 51 million visitors in 205 days. Because of the great distance between the Pont de l'Alma and the Pont d'Iéna, the organizers decided to build a footbridge between the two. Designed by Jean Résal, the architect of the Pont Mirabeau and the Pont Alexandre-III, the footbridge was inaugurated on April 13, 1900 – the day before the opening of the exposition. It was supposed to be destroyed afterwards, but they decided to keep it up. In 1906, it was moved a few dozen meters upstream. Landmarked as an historical monument in 1966, it was since repainted in *bleu de Paris*, or "Paris blue."

Address Between Avenue de New-York and Quai Branly, 75116 Paris | **Getting there** Metro to Iéna (Line 9) or RER to Pont de l'Alma (Line C) | Tip On the Rive Gauche, follow the Seine upstream to Pont de l'Alma. This is the beginning of the Berges, a pedestrianized stretch of the Left Bank that was opened in 2013. Over two kilometers long, it is one of the most popular spots in the capital, with "floating" gardens, deck chairs, napping cabanas (*les cabanes Zzz*), and outdoor dances in the summertime.

84__ The Passy Reservoir
To the water of Paris

From Rue Copernic, you will not notice much except the very tall walls. But go through the wide vaulted entry, up a spiral staircase, and there you will find the "reserve" basin, full of frolicking fish. Go up the next staircase – this one steep and made of iron – and you will find two more basins, these ones much larger.

The Eau de Paris city management company handles a two-tiered water network installed in underground tunnels, of which about 90% can be reached by foot. Paris' water system has been around since the end of the 19th century, consisting of 1,360 miles of canals conveying drinking water, and 1,050 miles conveying non-potable water.

The construction of the network of tunnels was overseen by Haussmann during the time of Napoléon III. But we have Eugène Belgrand – engineer of the department of bridges and roads, and service director of waters and sewers – to thank for this revolutionary project. Begun in 1858, the construction of the Passy reservoir took eight years to complete. Originally, five basins were planned – two open-air and three underground. In 1898, a third open-air basin was drilled. Called the Copernic basin, it was the largest, able to hold 760,000 cubic feet of water. In total, the capacity of the Passy reservoir exceeds 2.3 million cubic feet.

And what good is the non-potable water to Paris? It feeds into lakes and the waterfalls of the Bois de Boulogne and the Bois de Vincennes, to water the parks and public gardens, and to clean the streets and treat the sewer of the capital. The visit will also take you into the upper and lower Villejust basins, which are both empty now. The first is found underneath a huge lawn, and you will have to go down underground to get into the second basin, which is 370,000 cubic feet. With its arched vaults and sharp diagonals, it looks like an underground cathedral. It is a pretty fascinating place.

Address 26 Rue Copernic, 75116 Paris, www.eaudeparis.fr | Getting there Metro to Victor Hugo (Line 2) | Hours Free guided visits organized by Eau de Paris as part of the Parcours de l'Eau program, reservation required via website. | Tip After the undrinkable water, how about some of the drinkable variety? Head to Square Lamartine to fill up your water bottle with the pure stuff – straight from Passy! Drilled in 1886, it is 1,925 feet deep, and the only basin still in use! People come from far off to fill up their bottles and canteens: water from Passy is rich in iron, and has always been known for its health benefits.

85 __ Peach Walls of Montreuil

Where the peaches are just peachy

The Peach Walls of Montreuil are ripe with history, and an association is working hard to maintain them. Try to spot them from up on the Plateau du Haut Montreuil. Since the 17th century, the peach-tree farmers of what was then a village in the middle of the countryside were so famous for their work, they were known simply as *les Montreuil.*

They are the ones who figured out how to cultivate peaches on trellises. The method consists of leaning the peach trees up against plaster walls (made of gypsum extract from nearby quarries). The reflection of sunlight off these walls, along with the use of marl from the subsoil, enabled farmers to produce peaches whose reputation became world-famous.

In their heyday, the farmers of Montreuil were producing peaches of an exceptional size, weighing up to 14 ounces. They were destined for kings, served at Versailles under Louis XIV, and at the tables of the English and Russian courts, too.

In fact, there is a little spat between Versailles and Montreuil as to which city invented the trellis technique. Those in Versailles believe it was La Quintinie, the creator of the Potager du Roi, who invented the method; those from Montreuil believe it was their own Nicolas Pépin, a descendant of a long line of farmers, who came up with it in the 18th century.

At their peak in the second half of the 19th century, the *murs à pêches* covered more than a third of the city and produced over 15 million fruits. But at the beginning of the 20th century, Montreuil peaches were met with some tough competition from Provence, where the fruits ripen earlier and can be cultivated in larger quantities. That, along with real estate costs, the rise in the price of plaster and labor, sealed the fate of the Montreuil Peach Walls. But they still exist today, if only as a landmarked stretch of 21 acres at the end of the Impasse de Gobétue.

Address Association Murs à pêches (MAP): 77 Rue Danton; plots: Impasse de Gobétue, 93100 Montreuil-sous-Bois, +33 (0)1 48 70 23 80 | **Getting there** Metro to Mairie de Montreuil (Line 9), then bus 122 to Saint-Just | **Hours** Visits every Sun 2:30pm – 4:30pm | **Tip** Xavier Guicheteau, one of the growers, sells at the Marché sur l'eau (see ch. 72).
Originally from Gressy in Seine-et-Marne, he's one of the only growers in Île-de-France to cultivate his orchards in the old-fashioned "Montreuil" way. To keep the peachy theme going after your visit, hit up the Café La Pêche. It is the perfect snapshot the little city's scene, and it hosts music concerts that all sorts of people come to see (16 Rue Pépin, 93100 Montreuil, +33 (0)1 71 86 29 00, www.lapechecafe.com).

86__Le Père Magloire

Cemetery prankster

I have always loved roaming around cemeteries: basking in the silence, paying implicit homage to all those names, known or unknown. In the Cimitière de Charonne, there's one guy I have gotten to know quite well, François-Eloy Bègue – otherwise known as Magloire.

He cuts a mean figure, that Magloire. With his aged bronze silhouette, he is pure gentleman: cocked *bicorne* hat on his head, cane in hand, right under a chestnut tree at the top of the cemetery.

It practically rains chestnuts in autumn!

And don't fall for the end of the epitaph that adorns the base of the statue: "Here lies / Bègue, called Magloire / House painter / Patriot, poet / Philosopher and secretary / to Monsieur / de Robespierre / 1793." In truth, Magloire was never secretary to Robespierre! It was the Commission du Vieux Paris that, while doing its research on this gentleman, discovered this whopper. What's more, the statue atop Magloire's tomb was found by one of his friends – it does not look anything like the man underground.

Magloire was actually a house painter, which meant he was able to save up a small fortune during his lifetime. But mostly he was known for dancing at the Charonne *guingettes*, or outdoor dance halls.

Before he died in 1837, he asked his friends to make sure his burial was a festive one. They say that his friends put a liter of wine in his tomb and sang this song: "We must sing to the glory / of Bègue François-Eloy / A rare and sincere friend / Who in his last will and testament / Asked to be buried with all of us singing / To celebrate that he was a *bon vivant* / He left us each five francs. / As true friends of Magloire / Let's pour some wine and then toast / Let's drink together to his memory. / It is in honor of his death / That he ordered this meal."

Created in 1807, the Charonne cemetery is one of the only parish churchyards of the capital to be nestled right around its church.

Address Cimetière de Charonne, 119 Rue de Bagnolet, 75020 Paris, +33 (0)1 32 71 40 66 | Getting there Metro to Porte de Bagnolet (Line 3) | Hours Mon–Fri 8am–6pm, Sat 8:30am–6pm, Sun 9am–6pm | Tip At 102 bis Rue de Bagnolet, Flèche d'Or is a popular café-concert hall. It is located in the former train station of the village of Charonne – a history hinted at not so subtly by the amazing locomotive that sits on top of the bar!

Ycy repose
Bègue dit Magloire.
Peintre en bâtiments
Patriote, Poète.
Philosophe et secrétaire
de Monsieur
De Robespierre
1795

87 Le Pharamond Restaurant

Tripes à la mode de Caen

I have always loved the restaurants and cafés that opened right on the brink of the 20th century. Le Pharamond is one of them, and it does not disappoint. Its location is prime – right in Les Halles, an area teeming with new energy these days thanks to La Canopée, an enormous curving metallic structure covering the spaces Les Halles market once occupied.

In 1832, Alexandre Pharamond opened a stall in Les Halles selling *tripes à la mode de Caen*, or tripe stew, a specialty of his native Normandy. In 1879 he expanded, opening his own restaurant called À la Petite Normandie at 24 Rue de la Grande-Truanderie. But he didn't stop there. Instead he started a factory so that he could sell his beloved dish all over France. At Le Pharamond, the Paris-Normandie menu offers other Norman specialties, like andouillette sausage and veal filet.

At the end of the 19th century, Paris was buzzing with the success of its World Fairs. In 1898, Pharamond decided that for the Fair of 1900, he would completely redecorate his restaurant. Since then, the interior has been decked out in intricate woodwork, painted mirrors, and glass paste sculptures in the shape of fruits, vegetables, plants, and, of course, cooking pots filled with boiling tripe! All of it is fabulous, especially the little salons on the third floor, which you can reserve for a small fee.

There used to be a secret entrance to let famous people sneak in unobserved – Georges Clemenceau, Ernest Hemingway, Lino Ventura, Coluche, François Mitterand, the list goes on.

In 1988, the restaurant was listed in the inventory of historical monuments, and the following year, it was fully landmarked. Today, the gangsters who gave their name to the street – a *truand* is a thug or a mobster – have been replaced by fashionistas taking a *pause-café* in between the heavy-lifting reps of shopping the neighborhood boutiques.

Address 24 Rue de la Grande-Truanderie, 75001 Paris, +33 (0)1 40 28 45 18, www.pharamond.fr | Getting there Metro to Étienne Marcel (Line 4) | Hours Every day noon–3pm and 7pm–10:30pm | Tip I strongly recommend the Épicerie G. Detou. It is an incredible old-fashioned spot, good enough to humble the best pâtissiers (58 Rue Tiquetonne, open every day except Sunday 8:30am–6:30pm, +33 (0)1 42 36 54 67). Just next door, the other G. Detou boutique is a fine grocery store.

88＿Les Piaules

For backpackers in the know

This relatively new youth hostel called Les Piaules (which means "The Rooms" or "The Pads") opened with a buzz in October 2015. The excitement was in part thanks to its roof terrace, where four double rooms have access to an amazing panorama. You wake up to an unobstructed view: on one side the heights of Belleville, on the other the Sacré-Cœur cathedral of Montmartre, the Eiffel Tower, and even the La Défense towers. Not counting all the incredible rooftops and little chimneys that are, as everyone knows, what tourists in Paris love looking at best.

Les Piaules was the brainchild of three globetrotters: Matthieu Bégué, Damien Börjesson and Louis Kerveillant. They were working in finance and dreaming of launching a start-up, when they decided to invest almost 8 million euros, with the help of La Région, to acquire this beautiful 1930s building right in the heart of Belleville, a multicultural neighborhood that has been undergoing amazing transformations in the past years.

To stand out from the crowd and beat the competition, the owners tried to give Les Piaules a real Parisian vibe – not only through the aesthetic, but also by privileging local suppliers. To this end, the bar-restaurant only offers food and beverages that are typically French.

And so, I'm going to drop my backpack in one of these *piaules* to see Paris in a new light – as a backpacker – which I have never done!

I'll have the choice of rooms, of which there are 162 over nine floors. I'll have to share with other travelers: most rooms have four bunk beds. But each guest has a personal locker with an outlet to recharge a computer or phone, not to mention Wi-Fi access. And so that you do not have to use your neighbor, they've installed a punching bag in the common room.

Address 59 Boulevard de Belleville, 75011 Paris | **Getting there** Metro to Couronnes
(Line 2) | **Tip** One Thursday night per month, from 6:30pm–10pm, Le Food Market sets
up on the sidewalks of Boulevard de Belleville, between the Ménilmontant and Couronnes
Metro stations. Big tables and cuisines from around the world (www.lefoodmarket.fr).

89 Pierre Emmanuel Garden
Nature in all its liberty

Let's say you are exploring the 20th, one of my favorite arrondissements. After all that trekking up and down the hilliest of neighborhoods, a little break is just what you're bound to need. Try the Jardin Naturel, one of the most romantic gardens in Paris, which was recently renamed by the City Council in honor of the poet Pierre Emmanuel (1916–1984), born Noël Mathieu. A resistance fighter, a defender of the rights of man, and since 1968 a member of Académie française, Emmanuel was also a founder of the Maison de la Poésie in Paris.

Opened in 1995 and over 67,000 square feet, the natural garden has adhered since its inception to strict rules of maintenance: no regular mowing, no watering, minimal pruning, and respecting the cycles of vegetation. That is how it has allowed for the revival of the indigenous plants that once flourished when Charonne was still the countryside. Several habitats have been recreated – a real prairie, an enclosed pond, hedges, and a shaded wood. Under the oak trees, the maples, the cherries, and other nut trees, you will find ferns and the bellflowers you can recognize by their bluish-purple color. On the southern wall is a latticework of various climbers: vines, clematises, creepers with their downy flowers, and hops with their acrobatic stems that are used to perfume beer.

The pond is trimmed in white wicker plants, also known as basket willows because their thinnest branches are often used to weave baskets. You will also see mothers with strollers, sitting on benches to soak up the sun in a moment of calm. The natural garden also attracts many photographers, who love to zoom in on the wild flowers blooming all over the place. This little haven of nature is a favorite for all sorts of people – a throwback to the wildlife of pre-industrial Paris.

Let's cross our fingers and hope that the natural garden stays for a long time yet to come.

Address Access via Rue de la Réunion or Rue de Lesseps, 75020 Paris | Getting there Metro to Alexandre Dumas (Line 2) | Hours Mon–Fri from 8am; Sat & Sun from 9am, closes either at 5pm or 8:30pm depending on the season | Tip There is a great Thai restaurant nearby called Jardin d'Or. They make great family-style cuisine at reasonable prices that is a favorite of neighborhood residents (81 Rue des Pyrénées, open every day).

90 The Pontoise Pool
An almost-midnight swim

Everybody says that Paris comes to life at night, and here's a place that proves it. If you've ever tried to go get a few laps in after work, you will know how hard it is to find a pool that is open at night.

Well, here's the exception to that rule. The Pontoise pool, which owes its name to the street where it is found, stays open until 11:45 (except on weekends). An almost-midnight dip in the pool is possible right in the middle of Paris!

Built in the early 1930s and landmarked since 1998, the Pontoise pool is a rather unexciting place in terms of architecture, but that is what gives it its charm. All of the changing rooms are organized over several floors around the 36-yard pool, and from each you can access the pool directly. It feels like being on the gangways of a big ship! And just like during La Belle Époque, you can leave your things in a changing room and a *cabinetier* attendant will come let you back in once you're finished swimming. This charming feature might strike you as a bit outdated, but isn't it nicer than the cold hard lockers of most changing rooms?

The skylight ceiling makes for some great sunlight during the day, but at night, it is the lighting of the pool that really makes the place shine. And the music they play for night swims adds a nice touch to this totally unique pool.

Some people will tell you that the pool is a known meetup for gay men, but above all it seems to be a place for swimming fanatics. Be careful not to go into their lane if you're not the best swimmer: you might get elbowed in the face if you fall out of sync with their fast-paced rhythm. If you count yourself as one of them, however, try out the lane with the counter-current jet to turn up the dial on your swim. The place also has a workout area that is open just as late. The perfect way to become one of those famous nightcrawlers of Paris, right?

Address 19 Rue de Pontoise, 75005 Paris, +33 (0)1 55 42 77 88, www.carilis.fr | Getting there Metro to Maubert Mutualité (Line 10) | Hours Mon–Fri 10:15pm–11:45pm; daytime and weekend hours can be found online. | Tip For a while now, the Pontoise pool hosts "AquaCiné" nights, where you can come watch old classic film with your feet in the water, or while stretched out on a pool float! Information and reservations by telephone. Note: The Pontoise Pool has strict rules about swimwear. Everyone must wear caps and goggles. Men must wear competition style bathing suits. Board shorts are not considered swimwear, and you will not be permitted to use the pool.

91 __ The Public Baths

Showers for all at this bastion of public hygiene

In Paris, there are still real public bathhouses – and you might even say they're victims of their own success. Built in the name of public hygiene in the mid-19th century, the baths took off around the 1930s, especially in working-class neighborhoods. So it was for this one on Rue des Haies (in the 20th arrondissement), which dates from 1928, and which – exceptionally for the period – was a bathhouse tout court, and not a part of a public pool. From 1950 to the end of the 1990s, the public bathhouses were largely empty. But since entry became free in 2000, the 17 establishments in Paris have been topping one million showers per year.

The *bains-douches* or "B.D." on Rue des Haies is one of the most popular, with 7,500 visitors per month. Armed with toiletries, two or three times a week, men and women of all ages and classes cross the threshold of this art deco building of red brick and concrete, with an ornate ceramic-tile façade and a beautiful oval awning.

The establishment, now landmarked as an historical monument, was renovated in 2015. After passing through the dressing room, you dive into a universe of white smelling faintly of disinfectant. Each of the 49 stalls has a shower, a seat, and a mirror. You write your arrival time on a small chalkboard on the door and then have 20 minutes before the stall is rinsed and squeegeed.

About three quarters of the clients are men – some of which are homeless. But there are also students, the retired, the elderly, women, and families. Family stalls are equipped with two showers, two benches, and a mirror. Many clients have showers at home, but they may be too small, perhaps the faucet is broken, or hot water is too expensive, or maybe it is just more comfortable at the *bains-douches*. When it is crowded, you might have to wait up to 45 minutes on Sundays, for example, when the public baths close at noon.

Address 27 Rue des Haies, 75020 Paris, +33 (0)1 43 70 44, www.paris.fr | **Getting there** Metro to Buzenval (Line 9) | **Hours** Tue–Sat 8am–5pm; Sun 8am–noon | **Tip Walk** along Rue des Vignoles with its 15 culs-de-sac. There are flamenco classes at number 33, which is also home to the CNT-F (Confédération Nationale du Travail), and at number 95 you will find the last carpenter left in the neighborhood.

92 La REcyclerie

An urban farmhouse

Humans are contradictory creatures. Ever since I moved to the big city – a very long time ago – I have done nothing but try to escape to the countryside at every possible moment! So it was with great pleasure that I discovered La REcylcerie, housed in the old Gare Ornano de la Petite Ceinture, which was put into service in 1869 right at the top of the 18th arrondissement. There is life, a communal vegetable garden, lots of pansies, aromatic plants, and free-range chickens laying real eggs.

Inside the farmhouse (painted bright red, possibly because the decorator is named Pierre Ferrari!), you will think you are back in the 1960s. Formica tables and chairs in every color face the big wall of windows that looks out onto the old train station platforms.

At the entrance to the right, you will find the atelier of René *le bricoleur* (the handyman) who can fix just about anything you bring to him. He is also available to teach his skills to complete idiots (great for me!), and he'll even lend you his tools. They offer gardening classes as well. At the cafeteria, there is soup at noon and in the evening if you want it.

At La REcyclerie, they're all about locavorism: all their produce is sourced from as nearby as possible, and much of it comes from the onsite *ferme urbaine*, or urban farm. They've also mastered the fine art of minimizing waste: wine, for example, is stored not in bottles but in vats. Whether you prefer white, red, or rosé, it is served on tap, just like in the good old days. Whichever grape you choose, you can be sure it is a local wine. And if you prefer to take your breakfast or lunch to go, head to Corner, where they'll whip up your orders in a jiffy, for very reasonable prices.

And if the approach here appeals to you in general, you can even become an Ami REcycleur by joining the association of the same name.

Address 83 Boulevard d'Ornano, 75018 Paris, +33 (0)1 42 57 58 49, www.larecyclerie.com | Getting there Metro to Porte de Clignancourt (Line 4) | Hours Open every day 7am–12am | Tip The old Gare de Saint-Ouen train station is turning into a hotspot. Three friends have rehabilitated the place and turned it into a theater, artists' atelier, and gourmet bistro, poetically called Le Hasard Ludique (The Funny Fate) (128 Avenue de Saint-Ouen, Metro to Porte de Saint-Ouen or Guy Môquet (Line 13)).

93_La Route du Tibet

The only Tibetan bookstore in Paris

In the shadow of the Panthéon, up on the Sainte-Geneviève Mountain, sits Paris' "Little Tibet." At first you may not even notice it: the rather discreet Tibetan boutiques melt easily into the Parisian landscape, but they are there, waiting to be discovered, and waiting to transport you to the "rooftop of the world."

Why not make La Route du Tibet bookstore your first stop? It is without a doubt one of the smallest shops in Paris, definitely one of the most charming, and it also happens to be the only Tibetan bookshop in the capital!

Before it was a bookstore, it was a crafts store opened in 1982 by three young Tibetan refugees who'd arrived in Paris on academic scholarships from the French government. Not wanting to leave once their studies were finished, they threw themselves into an adventure with a two-fold goal: on the one hand, they wanted to help French people discover Tibetan culture, which wasn't well-known here at the time. On the other hand, they hoped to showcase the crafts of Tibetan refugees in India and Nepal, and to help these artists profit from their goods, as sales of their works constituted their sole means of income.

Thanks to their hard work, the three young refugees were so successful that in 1989, they moved their boutique to a bigger spot. The original space, meanwhile, became the bookstore. It is a total haven of calm and serenity. Hang around and leaf through a book – they have one on every possible subject: Buddhism, the history of Tibet, its traditional medicine, its clothing and dances from different regions, travel writings, photography collections. Everything is here! Even coloring books for kids, high-quality Tibetan incense, and plant-based medicinal products.

Don't hesitate to ask advice from Tenzin, who takes care of the bookstore. He'll be happy to help, or share his experiences and spiritual reflections with you.

Address 3 Rue des Fossés-Saint-Jacques, 75005 Paris, +33 (0)1 46 33 10 16,
www.laroutedutibet.com | Getting there RER to Luxembourg (Line B) | Hours
Every day except Sun 11am–7pm | Tip If perusing the shop works up your appetite,
cross to the other side of Rue des Fossés-Saint-Jacques to try the famous Tibetan
momos (steamed dumplings) at the Tashi Delek restaurant.

94 Rue des Immeubles Industriels

Hot water on every floor!

This little street was born of the imagination of the industrialist Jean-François Cail. His idea was to create a mini-world of buildings where factory workers could both work and live. His other idea was to introduce small-scale manufacturing into the city without making the buildings look like factories.

Constructed in 1872–1873 by the architect Émile Leménil, the 19 buildings on either side of this street are identical, save for the different colors of their cast-iron columns. They housed 2,000 workers, mostly carpenters and woodworkers, and they offers a fascinating look into the lives of factory workers in Paris at the end of the 19th century.

Underground, an enormous steam engine supplied the power to the 230 individual ateliers. These were located on the ground floor, the mezzanine level, and the second floor, and they all had big bay windows to let in as much light as possible. On the upper levels, the lodgings had all the modern luxuries, still rare for the time: hot and cold water, gas, and lights.

The Rue des Immeubles-Industriels won the gold medal at the 1878 World's Fair celebrating new technologies. The ensemble of buildings was listed as an historical monument in 1992. Beginning in the 1930s, Jewish immigrants, mostly from Poland, moved into the area and opened tailor shops. In 1941, when the raids started, young men joined the FTP-MOI, or *Francs-tireurs et partisans – main-d'œuvre immigrée*, a Resistance group of immigrant laborers organized to fight the Nazis. Among them was Marcel Rajman, who in 1943 tried to take down Julius Ritter, the organizer of the *Service du Travail obligatoire* (STO), or military draft. He was shot at 21 years old on Mount Valérien, on February 21, 1944. A plaque at building number 1 commemorates his legacy.

Address Rue des Immeubles-Industriels, 75011 Paris | Getting there Metro to Nation (Line 6) | Tip In the neighborhood there are other factory-worker enclaves. If you want more information on the history of this fascinating street, read Hervé Deguine's work, *Rue des Immebles-Industriels*, which is only sold at Nation Diffusion, 307 Rue du Faubourg–Saint-Antoine.

95 Rue Pavée Synagogue

An art-nouveau challenge, taken on by Guimard

Do you like art nouveau? I happen to go nuts for it. The gently curving lines, the vegetable and floral motifs – I find it all enchanting. But did you know that right in the Marais, there's a tall, curving, art-nouveau synagogue, designed by Hector Guimard himself? It is the only religious edifice the architect ever made.

In the 1900s, the Marais welcomed an influx of Eastern European Jews. Conflicts soon cropped up between the French Jewish community and the new arrivals, especially the Polish and the Russians, who were grouped together under the name of Agoudas Hakehilos. These latter eventually decided to branch out on their own, and in 1913, pitched their challenge to Hector Guimard: to build a synagogue on a narrow, crooked parcel of land of barely 1,000 square feet.

The talented architect rose to the occasion, breaking ground in June of the same year, with the synagogue's doors opening in October.

A former student of the École nationale supérieure des Beaux-arts, Guimard was greatly influenced by Viollet-le-Duc, then by Victor Horta, leader of the Belgian art-nouveau scene. Guimard finally forged his own path, before being quickly forgotten after his death, only to be rediscovered in the 1960s.

The synagogue is tall – 40 feet high – and its height is reinforced by narrow windows, and further emphasized by its pilasters. Its rather austere concave façade is finished in cut white stone over a reinforced concrete frame. But there is a certain waviness to the building at the same time. The interior goes all out in art-nouveau flair: swirls of plant life everywhere – a motif reprised on the glass windows. Guimard drew everything himself: the lighting fixtures, which look like tulips, the chandeliers, and the brackets. And he repeated those waves that enliven the façade on the pews inside. The Rue Pavée synagogue is always abuzz, even in its décor.

Address 10 Rue Pavée, 75004 Paris, +33 (0)1 42 77 81 51 | Getting there Metro to Saint-Paul (Line 1) | Hours Every day except Sat, 10:30am–5pm, visits by reservation | Tip La Boutique jaune de Sacha Finkelsztajn, recognizable by its bright yellow color, keeps the Yiddish tradition alive (which you will smell from outside) with its famous strudel and traditional breads (27 Rue des Rosiers, 75004 Paris, +33 (0)1 42 72 78 91, www.laboutiquejaune.fr, every day except Tue).

96__Rue Réaumur

An ode to iron and glass

Unveiled in 1897, Rue Réaumur is a lesson in urbanism, a hymn to modernity and to artistic creation within technical constraints. At the end of the 19th century, the city of Paris launched a façade competition for buildings with dual functions: commercial (textiles) and industrial (press and printing). In response, Rue Réaumur transformed itself into a dazzling example of creations bound to architecture of iron and glass, along with the less frequent use of stone.

The architects came up with enormous bay windows and bow windows encased in metal, which became a very popular style for buildings.

The façade of number 118 won a prize in 1900, and it is one of the most elegant on the street, with its art-nouveau-ish floral and vegetable motifs. Its immense walls of windows, which ensured as much light as possible into the ateliers, take up most of the building.

Number 116 won a prize in the competition of the City of Paris in 1898. As for numbers 82–96, they're the perfect example of a grand 19th-century department store, with their two-story wall of windows. From 1897, when the street was built, until 1960, it was home to À Réaumur, which generalized prêt-à-porter and mail order sales.

You should also check out the fabulous Félix Potin-designed rotunda at number 51, built in 1910. Newspapers once held a major presence on Rue Réaumur. Building number 100 housed the offices of *l'Intransigeant* from 1924, and *France-Soir* until 1980. At number 124, *Le Parisien Libéré* had its headquarters from 1944 to 1973. The building's iron structure has today returned to the beautiful pale green color of its 1905 origins, and it is open to visits during the *Journées du Patrimoine* holidays. For a bit of stargazing, go have a peek at number 118: the Adequat artist agency is in that building. You might just spot Bérénice Bejo, Léa Seydoux, Tahar Rahim, or Lambert Wilson.

Address Rue Réaumur, 75003 Paris | Getting there Metro to Réaumur-Sébastopol
(Lines 3 and 4) | Tip On the street perpendicular to Rue Réaumur, the Raymond Bar is a
witty little place that gives a nod to Raymond Barre, who was Prime Minister from 1976
to 1981. This former swinger's-club-turned-trendy-bar (open Tue–Sat) has maintained
its pole-dancing studio in the basement and its steam room covered in mosaic tiles (13 Rue
Dussoubs, 75002 Paris, +33 (0)1 40 28 95 11, Mon–Sat 6pm–2am).

97 __ Saint-Martin-des-Champs

The birth of the Gothic style in Paris

Some places have extraordinary destinies – like this church, for example. It was by turns a Merovingian basilica, a priory of the Order of Cluny, a hub for scientific experiments, and finally a museum gallery. The history of the Saint-Martin-des-Champs church has something for everyone, but it is loved especially by fans of medieval Gothic architecture, as it was the first Gothic church in Paris.

Today the church is part of the Musée des Arts et Métiers, and during 1990 renovations, Merovingian sarcophagi were discovered under its floor. Curious as to whether the spirits of this 6th-century necropolis run wild at night when the museum sleeps? Go find out; the place definitely has a mysterious vibe.

In the 6th century, the prosperous monks of the Order of Cluny installed themselves in this then priory, which at the time was situated outside the city walls of Paris (hence its bucolic name). If you look up, you will see that the arched vaults of the ambulatory are somewhat clumsily constructed – but that is what gives this once-rural church its charm. Built before the Saint-Denis Basilica (the paradigm of Gothic architecture), the Saint-Martin-des-Champs church bears witness rather to the 7th-century transition from the Roman to the Gothic style.

After the monks fled during the French Revolution, the church was granted a new life in 1802 with the opening of the Musée des Arts et Métiers, a scientific and technical museum. It became a gallery that showcased scientific experiments before an audience – a very popular attraction for Parisians at the time. The rails on the ground show the traces of this moment of history; they were the means through which little trolleys could run around the nave in order to transport the necessary elements for the science demonstrations. Foucault's pendulum (proving the rotation of Earth) still hangs to this day from the choir's chamber.

Address 60 Rue Réaumur, 75003 Paris, +33 (0)1 53 01 82 00, www.arts-et-metiers.net |
Getting there Metro to Arts et Métiers (Lines 3 and 11) | Hours Tue–Sun 10am–6pm,
Thu until 9:30pm (free from 6pm) | Tip If you go explore the collections at the Musée
des Arts et Métiers, look for the wild cat hiding in its walls. It looks almost realer than in
nature, and it is waiting for you to discover it in one of the rooms. Can you guess what it is
made of?

98 — Saint-Séraphin-de-Sarov Orthodox Church

The smallest church in Paris

From out front on Rue Lecourbe, you would never guess what is hiding on the other side. But open the carriage door, cross the first courtyard, and head towards the island of greenery that forms a second backyard. There is a little church tucked away back there, well protected from the chaos of city-dwellers.

The story of this Orthodox church begins not in Paris but far off in Russia, with the Revolution of 1917. The Russians who found refuge in Paris in its aftermath first came to Rue Lecourbe to visit the private mansion adjoining the church. Today, it is a parish house, but back then it was a place they could seek medical help and other services in their native tongue. Times were tough back then for the Russian refugees. In search of a place to gather, they were allowed to convert the garden shed into a little chapel, which to this day follows the tenets of traditional Russian Orthodox liturgy.

The garden-shed chapel was later transformed into the small wooden church that you see today. While the archpriest Dimitri Troïtsky founded the parish, the metropolitan archbishop was the one who consecrated the place to Saint Séraphin de Sarov (1759–1833). Canonized in 1903, the presence of Séraphin is signaled in the interior of the church by a painting with a large forest in the background, as the saintly man is known for having spent many years living as a hermit.

Over time, the church was expanded, but the neighboring trees of the original chapel were never disturbed. So instead of columns, it is tree trunks that surround this unique little house of worship – you won't find anywhere else like it! There are traces of Orhodox décor: the wall of icons separating the sanctuary from the nave features magnificent rare works made in the purest Russian tradition.

Address 91 Rue Lecourbe, 75015 Paris, +33 (0)6 62 65 75 04, www.seraphin.typepad.fr | Getting there Metro to Volontaires (Line 12) | Hours Sat from 5pm; Sun from 10am | Tip On the parish website, you can find the dates of open houses during good weather. These are a nice opportunity to discover not only the church but also the people who attend it.

99__Le Salon du Panthéon
Catherine Deneuve, decorator extraordinaire

Here is a special place: totally discreet, almost secret. It is located on a peaceful street in the Latin Quarter, just above the Panthéon cinema, a mythical theater where as a student I spent entire afternoons. There's nothing hinting at its existence; the Salon du Panthéon is an address for those in the know – those who won't even tell their friends about it!

As soon as you go inside, the tone is set by the size of the room: 1,600 square feet. You'd think you were in the loft of some trendy Parisian who happened to have hired Catherine Deneuve as interior decorator. In fact, decorating was one of the actress's first predilections. With assistance from the cinema decorator Christian Sapet, Deneuve has created an atmosphere that totally feels like a film set from the 1970s: parquet floors, blood-red carpet, sofas in black leather and red velvet. Deep armchairs and softly lit beautiful lamps add to the place's charm.

The Salon du Panthéon is great for lunch, teatime, or cocktails. Alternatively, you can rent the space for premiere parties, press junkets, brunches, cocktail parties, press conferences, showrooms. It can accommodate up to 200 people. It is also pleasant to sit outside on the terrace, with its wall tapestried in pots of flowers. And you can do it even when the weather is bad – the terrace is heated in winter.

Be sure to try the house chocolate cake, an all-around favorite, and to leaf through all the gorgeous books displayed on the shelves. The conversations are muted, the welcome is charming and the service is efficient. And don't forget – there is a movie theater right underneath you! Founded in 1907, the Cinéma du Panthéon is one of the oldest theaters in Paris. In 1930, it was the first to show films in their original version. *The Love Parade of Ernst Lubitsch*, with Maurice Chevalier singing and acting in English, was the first.

Address 13 Rue Victor-Cousin, 75005 Paris, +33 (0)1 56 24 88 80 | Getting there Metro to Cluny-La Sorbonne (Line 10) or RER to Luxembourg (Line B) | Hours Mon–Fri noon–7pm | Tip In the Latin Quarter, the Arènes de Lutèce (49 Rue Monge) are the last vestiges of the Gallo-Roman era, and thus the oldest monument in the capital. Free entry every day.

100__ The Sèvres Door

Sandstone in full force

Ever wander around Paris looking for a quirky place you have passed a million times without ever really registering it? I do it all the time – most recently with the Porte de Sèvres. Flattened against a perpendicular wall on Boulevard Saint-Germain, you will not necessarily spot it at first. But once you have – what a beauty!

In ceramic sandstone, this former city wall was one of the entries of the imposing French Manufacturers Pavilion at the World Fair of 1900. Built in the center of the Esplanade des Invalides, the building was one of the highlights of the exposition. Conceived by the architect Charles-Auguste Risler, with decorations by the sculptor Jules Coutan, the Porte de Sèvres is made of an arc framed by pillars supporting a cornice adorned with garlands and flowers. Above runs an entablature patterned with panels of sculpted foliage. The glass window that was supposed to be in the center was replaced by a backdrop with, in the middle, a medallion depicting a gracious female sculpture who herself is an allegory for ceramics. Underneath, on the bas-reliefs, you notice little potters at work.

The name "Sèvres" is inscribed above the door – that is some big-time publicity for the manufacturer, which had huge success at the Fair with its latest productions. On either side, there are two dates: 1753, the beginning of the construction of the Sèvres factory, and 1900, the year of the World Fair. An architect of several pavilions at the Fair, Charles-Auguste Risler was one of the principal collaborators with the Sèvres factory in the 1900s. He specialized in the use of ceramic sandstone, a material that is much more resistant than earthenware or enameled terracotta, and which lasts much longer. The excellent conservation of this beautiful door, whose tones have faded into gorgeous shades of blue and turquoise, can attest to the superior lifespan of ceramic sandstone.

Address Square Félix-Desruelles, 168 bis Boulevard Saint-Germain, 75006 Paris | **Getting there** Metro to Saint-Germain-des-Prés (Line 4) | **Tip** Have you ever tried the waffles from Chez Méert, which has been in Lille since the dawn of time? In 2013, Méert opened a Paris location that looks like a little jewel box. Try their most famous dish, the Madagascar Vanilla Waffle, whose recipe is a well-guarded secret! (3 Rue Jacques-Callot)

101 Skyline Bar and Lounge
Cocktails with a view

For a sunset and an amazing view of the west of Paris, there's no better place than the Skyline Bar & Lounge. On the 19th floor of the Hôtel Meliá, the most recent 4-star outpost that opened in February 2015 in the business district of La Défense, it is the only rooftop bar you can access in the neighborhood.

The building boasts a luxurious and innovative design, and it sits right on the Axe Historique Parisien (the stretch with the Arc de Triomphe). Its view spans the Seine, the Bois de Boulogne and the volutes of the Fondation Louis-Vuitton, the Eiffel Tower and the best of the Avenue des Champs-Elysées.

At the foot of the hotel, there's the Greek artist Takis' splendid 1988 installation called *Le Bassin*, a pool-like basin in which the Greek sculptor planted 49 luminous multicolored masts that sway with the wind. In 1991, Takis reproduced his piece called *Les Signaux* directly onto the esplanade at the back of the Grande Arche, not far from the Hôtel Meliá.

Since the La Défense neighborhood was launched in 1958, it has been a hotbed of contemporary architecture. It is also an open-air art gallery where nearly 80 large-scale works can be viewed, by the likes of Agam, Calder, César, Miró, and Moretti.

One of the most difficult to find is anonymous. It is a fragment of the Berlin Wall, 65 feet long and 10 feet high, and covered in original graffiti. It is mounted on glass panels, on which the names of about a hundred European cities are inscribed, symbolizing reunification. Since 1996, it has been installed in the Coupole-Regnault neighborhood. To get there, take the staircase to the left of the police station, before the passageway, and go down towards the Jules Verne Terminal corridor. Once you arrive at the platform level of the buses, all you have to do is cross the roundabout street of La Défense and go up a few steps.

Address 2 Esplanade du Général-de-Gaulle, 92400 Courbevoie, +33 (0)1 75 57 99 00 | **Getting there** Metro to Esplanade de la Défense (Line 1) | **Hours** 5pm–midnight | **Tip** Discover La Défense through the Defacto agency site, which organizes activities, events, and visits throughout the year. (www.ladefense.fr/sous-home/decouvrir-la-defense)

102__ Solar Hôtel
The world is organic

How fitting that I found this eco-hotel – the first in the capital – while searching for a bit of greenery in Paris! It is right near the Place Denfert-Rochereau and Rue Daguerre, and not too far from the Montparnasse station. And it is the perfect spot to spend the night.

Opened about twenty years ago and completely renovated in 2014, the place is never empty, probably because the cost of staying there is shockingly reasonable. The fixed price – the same for all the rooms – includes all services, including breakfast, bike rental, and computer rental.

The rooms are mostly white, with flashes of bright colors – turquoise, neon pink, orange. At breakfast, everything served is organic, from the jams to the butter. The bread and pastries come from the Moisan Boulangerie, and they even have Normandy orange juice.

There's the context. The philosophy of the hotel, as explained by Franck Laval, its director, encourages the elimination of individual packaging (probably the most wasteful part about staying in a hotel), and the use of biodegradable products. There's also a sort of signage system that is attention-grabbing, funny, but also informative. Its goal is to instill its clients with good eco-habits that they'll keep up once they're back home.

Back to the breakfast! In nice weather, you can have it in the garden, while admiring the flowers and listening to the birds. If you are not a total klutz, you can rent a bike from the hotel. You can also borrow a computer – but it can only be used in the common spaces, so that the Wi-Fi does not disturb the people sleeping in the bedrooms. If you want to relax, read, or just do nothing, the garden is also open for hanging out. You can even have a picnic there if you feel like it, or have friends come meet you. The director of the hotel hopes to develop other Solar hotels in Paris and the provinces. Let's hope he does so, and soon.

Address 22 Rue Boulard, 75014 Paris, +33 (0)1 43 21 08 20, www.solarhotel.fr | **Getting there** Metro (Lines 4 and 6) or RER (Line B) to Denfert-Rochereau | **Tip** There's no beating Chez Jean-Claude on Rue Vandamme! This new bar-restaurant, with its attractive turquoise façade, takes its inspiration from the Belgian actor's best lines to whip up cocktails and yummy menus: "One plus one = onze," "Double High Kick," etc. The cherry on top is that a little terrace can be found in the back of the restaurant. (9 Rue Vandamme, +33 (0)1 43 21 57 58, Tue–Sat noon–4pm and 6pm–1:30am)

103 Sorbonne Astronomy Tour

Stargazing in the city

In the middle of the big hill of the Rue Saint-Jacques, at the steepest part where it is hardest to go up on a bike, look up. From there you will be able to spot the astronomy tower of the Sorbonne, which stands 130 feet tall. The school was founded in the 8th century, before being completely rebuilt in 1900, except for the chapel. And its original vocation was as scientific as it was literary. The astronomy tower, which has come back to life since 1975, is proof of this heritage.

The address is kept secret, only known by those lucky enough to get in for the observation sessions organized by the Société astronomique de France (SAF). The tours cap out at groups of five people because of how cramped the spaces are, which is why you have to reserve a spot six months ahead of time. On a gorgeous night with clear skies and a full moon, I was lucky enough to get the chance to plunge my head into the stars during an observation session run by Francis Oger, a mathematician and the vice-president of the SAF. To get to the dome, we crossed the imposing main courtyard of the Sorbonne (where a few amphitheaters still had their lights on), took an elevator, and climbed several floors on a steep and narrow winding staircase.

On the way, I saw an optical workshop where workers were busy making telescopes and polishing lenses. Through the windows of the room, square like the tower itself, the 360-degree panorama is unforgettable (provided the weather is good and the pollution isn't too bad!). Once we made it to just underneath the dome, which weighs about seven tons but which my guide managed to get open with a few yanks on the pulley, I put my eyes to the antique telescope from 1935 and looked right up at the Epsilon Lyrae star system.

Afterwards, I had stars in my eyes and on my mind. No doubt that since then, I have been looking at the Parisian sky differently.

Address 17 Rue de la Sorbonne, 75005 Paris, +33 (0)1 42 24 13 74 (for reservations), www.saf-sorbonne.eu | Getting there Metro to Cluny – La Sorbonne (Line 10) | Hours By reservation only | Tip You can visit the Sorbonne by appointment, Mon – Fri and one Sat per month. For access for people with reduced mobility or physical handicaps, call +33 (0)1 40 46 23 48 or write to visites.sorbonne@ac-paris.fr.

104__Le Spa "Dans le Noir?"
A spa in the dark

You are not afraid of the dark, *and* you like new experiences? Or maybe you are afraid, but you're dying to confront that fear? Whatever your situation, it is worth checking out the "Dans le Noir?" spa, because its gimmick is actually a totally transformative experience. Sure, you like massages, but have you ever had one "in the dark?"

As soon as you enter the spa, located in the heart of the Montorgeuil neighborhood, just behind Les Halles, you are taken under the wing of a therapist who is either blind or visually impaired – whence the place's name. They will lead you through this unknown world – do not worry, there's soft lighting at first to help you make your way through the shadows, but eventually you will find yourself in total darkness.

According to the massage you chose, the expert hands of these blind masseurs will work on your face or your body. And since you cannot see anything, your other senses are sure to be on high alert, making you much more sensitive to sounds, smells, and to the touch of the massage itself.

It is a completely novel way of experiencing your environment, and it feels good. It is also an interesting role reversal. In general, you are the one helping a blind person cross the street, or read a sign, when they are unable to do so. But here at the spa, their non-visual talents kick into gear. Let yourself go, trust your body and the person in control of it – you will be so relaxed, you will practically taste the ambiance.

The spa also offers couples' massages, which is a nice way to try out the whole experience of total darkness. And you might as well take advantage of the steam room before your massage starts. It is a gorgeous space, with its beautiful starry sky, which you can even rent out for private events like bachelor or bachelorette parties. In short, the spa is sure to be a hit with anyone who likes their pleasures on the quirky side.

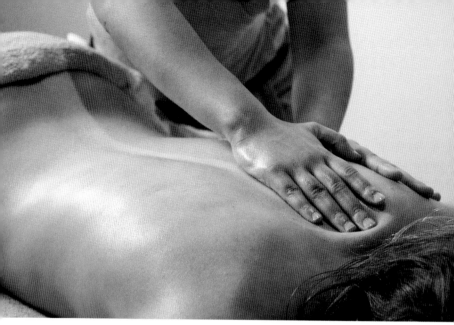

Address 65 Rue Montmartre, 75002 Paris, +33 (0)1 83 95 46 77, www.lespadanslenoir.com | Getting there Metro to Sentier (Line 3) | Hours Mon – Fri noon – 8pm, Sat 10am – 8pm, some Thursday nights (*les nocturnes jeudis*) until 9pm | Tip Have your ever tried eating in total darkness? At first it is disorienting – you cannot see anything or anyone, and you lose your bearings. Here, the surprise menu is also served by the blind or visually impaired. Another trippy experience that sharpens the senses. (Dans le noir? 51 Rue Quincampoix, 75004 Paris, +33 (0)1 42 77 98 04)

105__ Square de la Roquette
The doors of the penitentiary

The two sentry boxes at the entry to the Square de la Roquette recall the more tragic days of French history. They're vestiges of the former Roquette prisons, built in 1830 and 1836 on either side of the street. The first, called Petite Roquette, was reserved for young convicts. The second, called Grande Roquette, was a *dépôt de condamnés*, or a "depot" for the condemned awaiting either prison time or the death penalty. The latter didn't have to walk more than a few steps to start their final voyage as, from 1951 on, the guillotine was installed on five slabs of stone right at the entry of the prison. You can still see them, encrusted in the asphalt of the road, at the intersection of Rue de la Roquette and Rue de la Croix-Faubin.

The Grande Roquette also undertook the killing of hostages by the *Fédérés* during the Commune de Paris in 1871. But shortly after the last execution, on February 2, 1899, it was closed and demolished.

The Petite Roquette, meanwhile, stayed open. The writer Jean Genet, an orphan and a young delinquent, was imprisoned there during three months in 1925, at the age of 15, before being sent to a "camp" (more like a prison for children) near Tours. From the 1930s on, it was reserved for women. Later, as the stone inscriptions attest, 4,000 women resistance fighters were jailed here from 1940 to 1944 for having battled against the occupiers.

Both Roquetttes were demolished in 1975 and gave way to a square. The space itself was the site of another piece of history – that of Olympe de Gouges, the pioneer of feminism born in 1748, after whom the cultural center in the basement is named. The author of the *Déclaration des droits de la femme et de la citoyenne* (1791) was accused by the Jacobins of neglecting her domestic duties to get mixed up in politics, and was guillotined in 1793, at the height of the Reign of Terror.

Address 143 Rue de la Roquette, 75011 Paris | **Getting there** Metro to Voltaire (Line 9) | **Hours** Mon–Fri from 8am; Sat–Sun from 9am; (seasonal closing times) | **Tip** The Musée du Fumeur (museum of the smoker) is an incredible place with an anti-tobacco agenda, a bookstore-gift shop, a gallery, several exhibitions – and a vaping salon. (7 Rue Pache, every day except Sun, noon–7:30pm, bookstore-gift shop free)

106__The Street Art
of Montreuil

An open-air art gallery

The Street Art movement that made its début in France in the 1980s now has its own celebrities – Espion, Invader, Artof Popof, Nemo, Mosko and associates and Jérôme Mesnager, to name a few.

The little city of Montreuil has a great deal going on. It counts almost 800 working artists living within its walls. So it is neither a surprise that this pioneer town has turned into an open-air art gallery, with more than 80 large-scale graffiti works, nor that it launched its first Street Art Festival in September 2015.

Artists of all expressive forms convene over two days of outdoor performances and exhibitions all over the city's walls, which are temporarily proffered by willing owners to host works of graffiti, stencils, mosaics, or stickers. Street art is by nature ephemeral, but the style of each artist is generally quite distinct and recognizable. On one wall you will find the works of plastic artist JBC, a resident of Montreuil, who mostly creates collages.

Further on to the right on the same wall, a fresco called *La Compagnie du cinématographe* recalls that this was once the site of Pathé film studios. Charles Pathé chose the former enclosed market, covered entirely in glass windows, because it was the perfect place to have studios that would be flooded with natural light throughout the year. The place still exists today, although Pathé outgrew it in 1928, when he handed it over to a metalworking company. Under the splendid glass windows, which were named historical monuments in 1997, these mythical studios have been brought back to life since 2002, when the site was transformed into artist ateliers and, once again, film studios. Studio Albatros, run by Lucien and Lily Chemla, has become a performing arts workshop for young artists, writers, dancers, designers and filmmakers.

Address 52 Rue du Sergent-Bobillot, 93100 Montreuil | **Getting there** Metro to Croix de Chavaux (Line 9) | **Tip** At this same address, the Studio Albatros can be visited on the *Journées portes ouvertes* (open house days) of the artist ateliers, on one of the first weekends of October, and during performances.

107__The Suresnes Vineyards

The little white wine of the west

Who knew that on the building-covered hillsides of Suresnes, every year they harvest a nice fruity little white wine? With its southeast exposure on the slopes of Mont Valérien, the Clos du Pas Saint-Maurice vineyard is the biggest in Île-de-France, stretching over just one hectare of land. Run by the municipality itself, it is the only one in the region that produces a wine for sale, and the vinification takes place right on the premises.

Each year, the 4,800 vine plants produce between 4,500 and 5,000 bottles of a semi-dry wine, made from 85% Chardonnay and 15% Sauvignon grapes. The presence of the vineyard is hinted at in the names of the streets, including Rue des Vignes, Impasse des Vignerons, Rue des Bons-Raisins, and Rue du Port-aux-Vins.

At the beginning of the Middle Ages, Suresnes was a small village of vintners: Nicolas de Hacqueville, who ran the Hôtel-Dieu hospital, had patients drink the wine for its curative properties. And until the 17th century, Suresnes wine was considered one of the best vintages of the Île-de-France. It was even served at the tables of royals. But in 1709, a harsh winter came along and destroyed all the grapes, so that the entire vineyard had to be replanted. By the 19th century, the vineyard was back in action, producing a *p'tit bleu* made from black grapes, and an excellent white, both of which were the drink of choice in the *guinguettes* dance halls.

In 1926, the mayor of Suresnes, Henri Sellier, managed to save the vineyard at a time when the area was giving way to rapid urbanization. Other mayors followed his lead, and today the white wine of Suresnes continues to make residents and tourists alike very happy. After all, there's always a reason to indulge: salons, flea markets, open house days for the galleries, not to mention the Festival des Vendanges, which takes over the streets of Suresnes at the beginning of each October.

Address 4 Rue du Pas-Saint-Maurice, 92150 Suresnes, +33 (0)1 40 99 13 17, www.suresnes.fr | **Getting there** RER to Suresnes-Mont-Valérien (Lines L and U) or tramway to Suresnes-Longchamp (Line 2) | **Hours** Visits and sales, Mon 2pm – 7pm | **Tip** Before getting on the tram back home, go through the door of MUS. The former Suresnes-Longchamp train station was transformed into a museum in 2013. There you will discover the history of the vineyard, but also of social urbanism, which took off in Suresnes between 1920 and 1940 thanks to Henri Sellier.

108__ Thaddaeus Ropac Gallery
The artsy suburbs

What do Paris and its suburbs do with their industrial heritage? Sometimes, they turn them into refuges for contemporary art! Will you dare to cross the Périphérique highway to check out the Thaddaeus Ropac Paris Pantin Gallery? It is a surprising discovery, both because it is a funny place to find an art gallery and because the quality of the works presented is superb. In fact, Pantin has become a pretty artsy spot, and it is definitely worth exploring.

The Thaddeus Ropac Gallery, founded in Salzburg, Austria in 1983, has had a presence in France since 1990, when it opened a location in the Marais. But in 2012, in search of bigger spaces to exhibit larger works, they set up shop in the suburb of Pantin. Close to the Parc de la Villette and the new Philharmonie de Paris, the choice of Pantin makes total sense, especially because its industrial past provides some incredible spaces, like this one, which was formerly a boiler manufacturer in the 19th century.

The brick buildings have been landmarked, and now that the four main spaces (which reach up to 40 feet high) have been renovated, they're perfect for showing monumental sculpture and large paintings. The lighting is exceptional thanks to the presence of skylights overhead – artists would be hard pressed to imagine a better setting for showing off their achievements. And there is no need to be a great specialist of contemporary art to appreciate the muted atmosphere of this gallery. After wandering quietly throughout the galleries, you are sure to want to come back again soon – and lucky enough, there are super exhibitions organized throughout the year.

Outside, there are lots of other spaces where concerts and conferences take place. And for food lovers, there is Café Bleu with a choice selection of sweets and treats – perfect to get yourself recharged before heading back to the city.

Address 69 Avenue du Général-Leclerc, 93500 Pantin, +33 (0)1 55 89 01 10, www.ropac.net/contact/paris-pantin | **Getting there** RER to Pantin (Line E) | **Hours** Tue–Sat 10am–7pm | **Tip** The Thaddeus Ropac de Salzbourg Galleries are a bit far, but the ones in the Marais are worth checking out as well. The experience is different but complementary: after the monumental works of Pantin, you will discover works of a more modest scale that are just as captivating at 7 Rue Debelleyme, 75003 Paris.

109__ The Tiki Lounge
Half-man, half-god

Who knew that even Parisians yearn to close their eyes and sway to the soft string music of Polynesian dreams? This Tiki Lounge, not far from the Canal Saint Martin, is like a trip to those far-off isles, via a layover in mid-century American nostalgia. Everything about the place – its décor, its cocktails, its music – is steeped in exoticism.

But who was this Tiki? Half-man, half-god, this venerated Polynesian figure is credited with the origin of humanity. According to the mythology of the Marquesas Islands of French Polynesia, Tiki arrived a long time ago from Hawaii, the home of the Gods, and created the first island in the archipelago. When the time came for Tiki to leave to create another island, an old wise man decided to make a statue in his image, so as to never forget him. And thus was born the first sculpture of Tiki!

Fast-forward to the 1950s, when Hawaii was integrated into the United States, and Americans were fantasizing about the islands of the Pacific. There, Tiki became a sort of pop-culture icon, and Tiki bars began popping up all over the country, from California to Florida. America in those days was a culture of productivity, but come Saturday night, they'd trade in that puritanical work ethic for wild times, dancing to Hawaiian tunes and downing exotic cocktails, one after the other.

Most of these are rum-based, which is not really a Polynesian speciality. The most famous is the Mai Tai, of course, which means "the best" in Tahitian. You're sure to find it on the menu at the Tiki Lounge, along with its virgin version, which tastes just as good.

The owner of the joint is a big fan of American rock'n'roll from the 1950s, along with the 1990s-era resurgence of Tiki kitsch. The lounge's Polynesian décor is without rival, and is ready and waiting just for you. Will you be able to resist the call of Polynesia, American-style?

Address 26 Rue de la Fontaine-au-Roi, 75011 Paris, +33 (0)1 55 28 57 72, www.tikilounge.fr | **Getting there** Metro to Goncourt (Line 11) | **Hours** Tue – Sat 6pm – 2am; happy hour 6pm – 8:30pm | **Tip** And if the desire to meet some real Tiki ancestors takes you, the Musée du Quai Branly presents a very beautiful collection of Oceanic art (37 Quai Branly, 75007 Paris).

110__ Vampires and Monsters Museum

I wasn't scared, I swear!

If you believe in monsters, vampires, werewolves, witches, demons, and fairies, then this unusual museum, founded by Jacques Sirgent, will suit you perfectly. Sirgent will welcome you into this home that has been in the family for a century. It was built in 1880 – which, as he notes, is precisely eight years after the series of murders attributed to Jack the Ripper, and seventeen years after Bram Stoker's *Dracula* was published. Obsessed with vampires since childhood, he's become an expert on the subject, as well as the author of several renowned works. More broadly, Sirgent is a specialist in the history of evil, giving talks in his museum and all over the world (usually dressed in black).

What he tells you will leave you speechless! As will the displays of terrifying objects – masks, hands, human heads, posters and paintings depicting famous satanic creatures. You will also see an anti-vampire kit dating from the 19th century, the typewriter used by Stoker and his author photo, along with photos of all the actors who have played Dracula on the big screen. Then there are the books – almost 1,500 rare works dating from the 16th century on, including the first French edition of Dracula, from 1919, and a video library of more than 1,000 films.

Funeral rites, sorcery, religions, witch-hunts – it is all covered by Jacques Sirgent, who sees these legends as the means through which humans were able to overcome fear of their environment. Evil is found in man, he says – not in vampires. Sirgent has also invented a remedy for children suffering from nightmares: he advises them to actively check under their bed for monsters, and if they find any, to talk to them or to trap them in a bottle. Alternatively, children can come to the museum to learn that vampires actually protect us from other *real* monsters. Nothing to be afraid of!

Address 14 Rue Jules-David (entrance through the back of the house), 93260 Les Lilas | **Getting there** Metro to Porte de Lilas (Lines 11 and 3bis) | **Hours** 10am–midnight with reservations by calling +33 (0)6 20 12 28 32 or +33 (0)1 43 62 80 76 | **Tip** Jacques Sirgent organizes thematic visits to the Père-Lachaise cemetery in French and in English on a daily basis. Visit www.museedvampiresetmonstresdelimaginaire.blogspot.fr

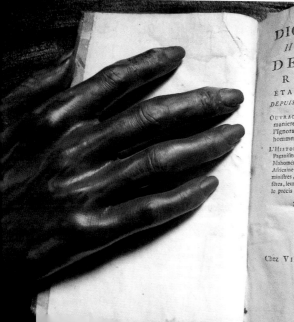

111 ZZZen Nap Bar
Bubbles of well-being

You have dreamt of a nap bar, haven't you? Well, they have made one – since 2011 the world's first nap bar has been open in the Passage Choiseul in Paris. No need to fight off that post-prandial fatigue at the office – just head over to the place where you have the right to abandon yourself into the arms of sweet slumber. If you are alive and working today, chances are your schedule is jam-packed and you have no free time. But there is nothing like a little nap to make you wake up (again) on the right foot!

The creator, Christophe Chanhsavang, knew the idea was bound to be a hit. His wife thought of it first, actually, after being inspired by her friend's successful opening of a wine bar. But here, you will only be offered tea to help you doze off. And Christophe is happy to enumerate the benefits of napping, which are recognized in workplaces around the world – though not yet in France, in spite of numerous studies proving its positive effect on the productivity of workers.

Convinced? No longer feeling guilty? Good. All that is left is choosing your type of nap: there's the hammock nap, the shiatsu bed with hot jade stones, or the anti-gravity armchair. They are all amazing, but here are our suggestions. For a real deep-sleep nap, the hammock and the shiatsu bed are perfect. With the soft music playing in the background, you're sure to drift off immediately. If you prefer an anti-stress massage that will relax your whole body, all the way to the tips of your fingers – and in record time – go with the anti-gravity armchair. The experience might sound overwhelming, but don't be shy about letting Christophe and his team guide you through designing a personalized program.

Finally, don't leave without taking advantage of the foot massage tools at your disposal. They are sure to help you wake up slowly and get back into the real world by putting your best, less-tired, foot forward.

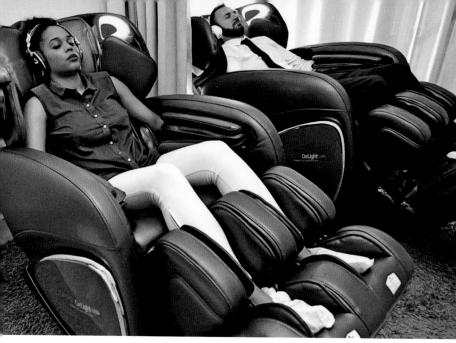

Address 29 Passage Choiseul, 75002 Paris, +33 (0)1 71 60 81 55, www.barasieste.com | Getting there Metro to Pyramides (Lines 7 and 14) | Hours Mon–Sat noon–8pm, reservation recommended | Tip Built in 1827, the Passage Choiseul is the longest covered passageway in Paris, and has recently been renovated. It has become the go-to spot for fans of Korean food, with several dining options attesting to this fact.

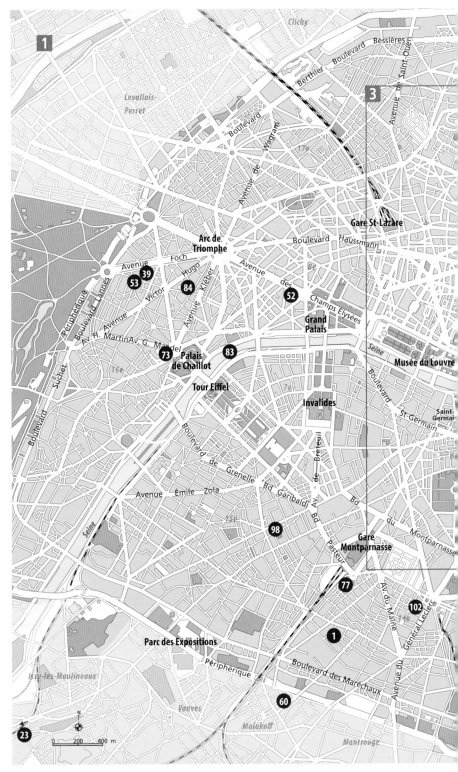

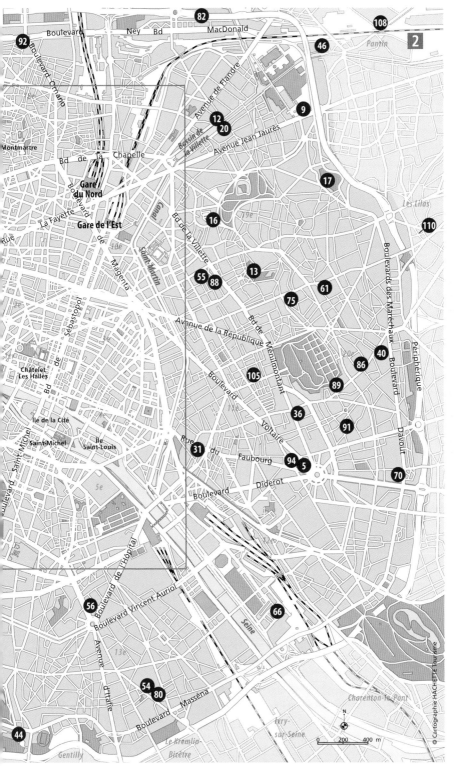

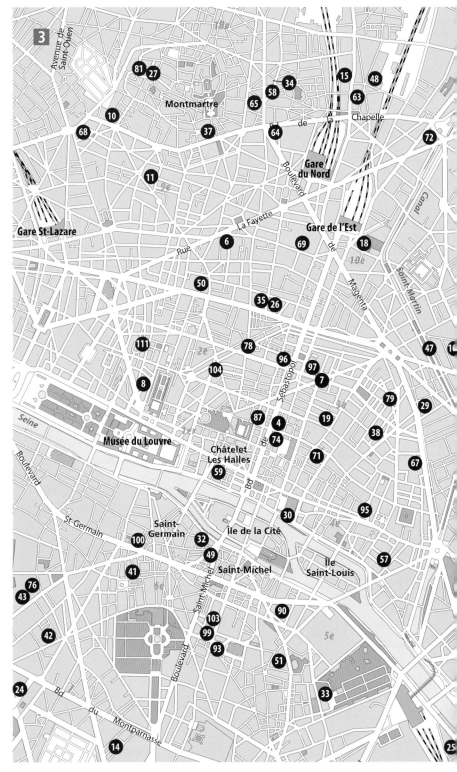

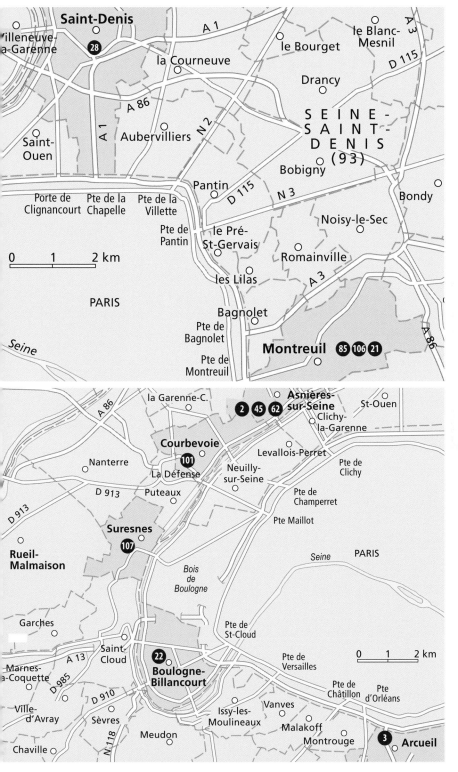

Lucia Jay von Seldeneck,
Carolin Huder, Verena Eidel
**111 PLACES IN BERLIN
THAT YOU SHOULDN'T MISS**
ISBN 978-3-95451-208-9

Rüdiger Liedtke
**111 PLACES IN MUNICH
THAT YOU SHOULDN'T MISS**
ISBN 978-3-95451-222-5

Frank McNally
**111 PLACES IN DUBLIN
THAT YOU SHOULDN'T MISS**
ISBN 978-3-95451-649-0

Rike Wolf
**111 PLACES IN HAMBURG
THAT YOU SHOULDN'T MISS**
ISBN 978-3-95451-234-8

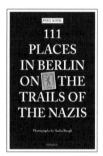

Paul Kohl
**111 PLACES IN BERLIN
ON THE TRAIL OF THE NAZIS**
ISBN 978-3-95451-323-9

Peter Eickhoff
**111 PLACES IN VIENNA
THAT YOU SHOULDN'T MISS**
ISBN 978-3-95451-206-5

Sharon Fernandes
**111 PLACES IN NEW DELHI
THAT YOU MUST NOT MISS**
ISBN 978-3-95451-648-3

Sally Asher, Michael Murphy
**111 PLACES IN NEW ORLEANS
THAT YOU MUST NOT MISS**
ISBN 978-3-95451-645-2

Gordon Streisand
**111 PLACES IN MIAMI
AND THE KEYS
THAT YOU MUST NOT MISS**
ISBN 978-3-95451-644-5

Dirk Engelhardt
111 PLACES IN BARCELONA
THAT YOU MUST NOT MISS
ISBN 978-3-95451-353-6

Rüdiger Liedtke
111 PLACES ON MALLORCA
THAT YOU SHOULDN'T MISS
ISBN 978-3-95451-281-2

Marcus X. Schmid
111 PLACES IN ISTANBUL
THAT YOU MUST NOT MISS
ISBN 978-3-95451-423-6

Stefan Spath
111 PLACES IN SALZBURG
THAT YOU SHOULDN'T MISS
ISBN 978-3-95451-230-0

Ralf Nestmeyer
111 PLACES IN PROVENCE
THAT YOU MUST NOT MISS
ISBN 978-3-95451-422-9

Christiane Bröcker,
Babette Schröder
111 PLACES IN STOCKHOLM
THAT YOU MUST NOT MISS
ISBN 978-3-95451-459-5

Beate C. Kirchner
111 PLACES IN FLORENCE
AND NORTHERN TUSCANY
THAT YOU MUST NOT MISS
ISBN 978-3-95451-613-1

Floriana Petersen, Steve Werney
111 PLACES IN SAN FRANCISCO
THAT YOU MUST NOT MISS
ISBN 978-3-95451-609-4

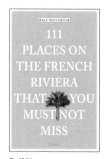

Ralf Nestmeyer
111 PLACES ON THE
FRENCH RIVIERA
THAT YOU MUST NOT MISS
ISBN 978-3-95451-612-4

Gerd Wolfgang Sievers
111 PLACES IN VENICE
THAT YOU MUST NOT MISS
ISBN 978-3-95451-460-1

Petra Sophia Zimmermann
111 PLACES IN VERONA
AND LAKE GARDA THAT
YOU MUST NOT MISS
ISBN 978-3-95451-611-7

Rüdiger Liedtke,
Laszlo Trankovits
111 PLACES IN CAPE TOWN
THAT YOU MUST NOT MISS
ISBN 978-3-95451-610-0

Gillian Tait
111 PLACES IN EDINBURGH
THAT YOU SHOULDN'T MISS
ISBN 978-3-95451-883-8

Laurel Moglen, Julia Posey
111 PLACES IN LOS ANGELES
THAT YOU SHOULDN'T MISS
ISBN 978-3-95451-884-5

Giulia Castelli Gattinara,
Mario Verin
111 PLACES IN MILAN
THAT YOU MUST NOT MISS
ISBN 978-3-95451-331-4

John Sykes
111 PLACES IN LONDON
THAT YOU SHOULDN'T MISS
ISBN 978-3-95451-346-8

Julian Treuherz,
Peter de Figueiredo
111 PLACES IN LIVERPOOL
THAT YOU SHOULDN'T MISS
ISBN 978-3-95451-769-5

Jo-Anne Elikann
111 PLACES IN NEW YORK
THAT YOU MUST NOT MISS
ISBN 978-3-95451-052-8

Authors

Renée Grimaud, the primary author of this guide-book, first came to Paris over forty years ago to study Classics, history, and art history, and has lived and worked here ever since. She is the author of many thematic and historical texts of the French capital. She has also collaborated on several guidebooks on Paris and Île-de-France.

Born in the heart of Paris, journalist **Sybil Canac** loves making new discoveries about her city, whether she's crossing it on foot, on her bike, or on the metro. She is the author of several books on the history and heritage of Paris. A dedicated Parisian for life, she also shares her findings on her blog: paris-de-toujours.over-blog.com.

Katia Thomas studied art history at the Sorbonne and began working as a guide in Paris in 2000. Since then, from neighborhood to neighborhood, from museum to museum, she's been traipsing all over the capital to discover its secrets and share them with others. The history and culture of the City of Lights continues to fascinate her!

Translator

Hadley Suter is a writer and translator living in New York. She teaches French at Columbia University and holds a Ph.D. from the University of California, Los Angeles.